Policies and Procedures
for
Your Organization

Build solid governance documents on any topic ...

... including cybersecurity

John Bandler

First edition published 2024

by John Bandler, 48 Wall Street, 11th Floor, New York, NY 10005

Copyright © 2024 John Bandler. All rights reserved.

ISBN-13: 978-1-963435-00-9 (paperback)

ISBN-13: 978-1-963435-01-6 (eBook)

ISBN-13: 978-1-963435-02-3 (hardcover)

Library of Congress Cataloging-in-Publication Data

Names: Bandler, John, author
Title: Policies and Procedures for Your Organization: Build solid governance documents on any topic ... including cybersecurity
Description: First edition. | New York, NY: John Bandler, 2024. | Includes appendix, references, index, glossary, resources and diagrams. | Summary: "Organizations need governance documents; policies, procedures, and other written rules that tell the organization and employees what to do and how to do it. These documents are an important part of management to help the organization comply with legal requirements, accomplish its mission and run efficiently. This book helps you and your organization build effective and quality governance documents to improve the organization and develop the individuals on your project team. This is for any type of organization and can be applied to any topic, and any type of governance document. Some chapters and sections are devoted to cybersecurity. Learn about the Five Components for Policy Work and Four Pillars of Cybersecurity." — Provided by publisher.
Identifiers: LCCN 2024903943 | ISBN 9781963435009 (paperback)
        ISBN 9781963435016 (eBook) ISBN 9781963435023 (hardcover)

Visit John Bandler's website at
  JohnBandler.com

Scan this QR code to go to the book page at
johnbandler.com/policiesbook/

DEDICATION

To my parents, wife, and children.
You make it possible and worthwhile.

CONTENTS

ABOUT THE AUTHOR

John Bandler actually read the policies and procedures that his prior employers expected him to follow. Now he runs his own law firm and helps organizations write their own policies and procedures.

He has written or improved many policies and procedures and has developed foundational concepts to build solid governance documents. He even built an online course devoted to cybersecurity policies and has researched the topic extensively. Now he brings you this book.

John is a lawyer, consultant, author, teacher, and speaker who helps individuals and organizations navigate today's risks. His areas of expertise include cybersecurity and cybercrime prevention, information governance, general governance, privacy, law, and more.

Before entering private practice John served in law enforcement for over twenty years as a police officer and then a prosecutor. He also served in the U.S. Army Reserve.

He earned his law degree from Pace University's Law School and his undergraduate degree from Hamilton College, majoring in Physics with a Computer Science Minor. Since graduating law school, he continues learning through self-study and every time he writes and teaches.

Some of his other works include:

- Cybersecurity for the Home and Office (2017 book)
- Cybercrime Investigations (2020 book)
- Corporate Cybersecurity Policies (online course)
- CIPP/US Certification Preparation Course (online course)
- Introduction to Law (online course)
- JohnBandler.com

John can be reached at:

John Bandler
Bandler Law Firm PLLC
Bandler Group LLC
48 Wall Street, 11th Floor
New York, NY 10005
JohnBandler.com
JohnBandler@JohnBandler.com

More about John at   johnbandler.com/about

ACKNOWLEDGMENTS

This book would not be possible without the help of many people over the course of my life and the writing of this book.

I will start with my wife, children, and parents, to whom I dedicated the book.

I also would like to acknowledge all the experts, mentors, supervisors, students, and clients who gave me knowledge, feedback, and experience throughout my life.

A thanks to those who helped on my first two books and many articles, whose editing suggestions now influence my writing. Readers, editors, co-authors, and publishers. And those who gave me the means to build courses in a variety of platforms, where I further developed my thinking and content. And especially to my cousin, Rob Bandler, former Deputy Director of IT Security at Cornell University, who read this book from cover to cover prepublication and provided valuable feedback (as he has done with each of my books).

I acknowledge my website JohnBandler.com, where I built many of these thoughts and words, where I can continually tweak my writings, diagrams, and thought process. I drew from there to write this book and refer the reader back there for more. The diagrams in this book are my creations and many early versions probably first appeared on my website.

Mostly, thank you, the reader. I never know who will read it and what their background or interests will be. I did my best to organize it well and write clearly. If you have constructive or positive feedback to share, please reach out.

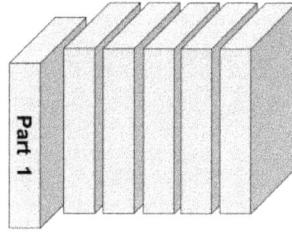

Part 1

A foundation
for better
policies and management

In this part

- Some policy foundations
- The Five Components for Policy Work

In other words:

- Let's pour a strong knowledge foundation we can build upon
- Learn what a typical house is made of and how to swing a hammer before you start building the house.
- Learn how a car works and sit behind the wheel and familiarize yourself with the controls before you start driving.

1

Why we need good policies and procedures

In this chapter:

- Why
- For who
- How
- Good principles
- Warnings and disclaimers
- Where you can find more (resources)
- Need a quick start guide? Check out Chapter 27

1.1 Why read this book?

Organizations need rules.

Some of those rules need to be written down.

This is what policies, procedures, and other governance documents are for.

If we are going to have written rules in our organization, they should be effective, clear, practical, and serve their purposes.

They should help us comply with legal requirements and achieve the mission of our organization.

They should help protect the organization, especially when the subject of the policies is cybersecurity.

This book enables you and your organization make that happen and improve the organization and project team members in the process.

1.2 Who is this book for?

This book is for anyone doing organization policy work—working on policies, procedures, and other governance documents that lay out organization rules or tell employees what to do. For documents on any topic at all because this process is foundational.

That said, I also have a few sections and chapters specific to cybersecurity.

This book can help the entire project team or be used as a guide by the project manager or document writers.

This book is also for everyone involved in organization management. Governance documents are an important part of management and at some point, management directives need to become rules and put in writing. Managers and leaders need to know how to build effective documents and improve their teams.

1.3 How to use this book

Use this book how it suits you.

Mostly there are two main ways people will read this.

First, it is written so that someone could read it all the way through from cover to cover, comprehensive and covering theory and details. Even if governance documents are not your passion, I hope the style keeps this readable and accessible. Maybe you have a few hours to read through the entire book as you prepare for a policy project or evaluate your organization management. Or you are thinking about how to improve your organization or your place within it. Read through and I hope you enjoy it and get some good ideas, knowledge, and skills.

Second, I worked to make it modular and well organized, since many readers want to go right to a particular topic. The table of contents, index, chapter beginnings, section headers and quick start guide can help you find what you need.

You can grab a pencil and mark it up as you go and there are extra pages for your notes.

I drop footnotes periodically because they serve a purpose when needed and it helps keep the main text streamlined.[1]

---

[1] Footnotes may provide a citation or reference when needed right then, though the end of each chapter will usually include chapter references and additional reading. Footnotes also include asides, vignettes, and minutiae which keeps the main text crisper. Skip it if you don't have the time, read it if they are of interest or a welcome diversion.

Some sections are marked as "preview" so you can have a brief summary on a topic where it fits within the sequence, but you also know it is covered in more detail later.

I also included a "quick-start guide". Your new electronics have a quick start guide and the concept works here too. Maybe you just want some quick tips and extra help on getting to the right place in the book. This quick start guide is located in Chapter 27.

1.4 Did you see about the quick start guide?

Just in case you missed it, Chapter 27 is the quick start guide!

1.5 My journey to write this book (preview)

For now, let's just say that I have thought about rules, policies, instructions, and laws for a long time, and this book is the result. If you have the desire to read about how this book came to be, you will find it in Chapter 28 (within Part 6, the "appendix"). I moved it there so we can get started with the main subject faster.

1.6 My policy resources on JohnBandler.com

My webpages on policies and procedures are among my site's top web search performers. I imagine an employee tasked with updating a company document and searching for something helpful on the internet– they find my site and one of my webpages.

The website was a way to publish and evolve my thinking, writing, and diagrams. Now this book evolves it further. I knew some would like a reliable book with everything put together, using comprehensive and cohesive philosophy that helps their organization for short and long term.

The website may have updates and is there for you as well.

1.7 Good principles scale up and down

As you read this book, remember that good principles can scale up and down. Every organization needs rules, but not every organization needs the same number of governance documents and same level of detail within each document. They should be tailored to the mission and needs of the organization.

While one size does not fit all, good principles as laid out in this book can be scaled to the right size for your organization.

1.8 Good principles translate across disciplines

Good principles about management and policies translate across domains, including cybersecurity, privacy, compliance, anti-money laundering, human resources, manufacturing goods, providing services, marketing, sales, and so on.

Different policies require consideration of relevant laws and practices and are for different audiences, but the fundamental principles on how to create and update them remain the same.

Most of this book is foundational and can be applied to any discipline. You just need to apply your own knowledge and research regarding the specific topic area.

A few sections and chapters are specific to cybersecurity so you can focus on them if needed or skip them if your current project is unrelated.

1.9 Cybersecurity

Some of you are working on a document project relating to cybersecurity and there are a few sections and chapters that are specific to cybersecurity, privacy, information governance, and cyberlaw. You can seek them out and dwell in these parts. The dedicated Chapters 19, 20, and 21 (all within Part 4) are all about cybersecurity.

Any cybersecurity section or chapter will have a "⏭" notation so you can press the fast-forward button (e.g., turn the pages) if your focus is different. They are there for another day.

Cybersecurity related documents are among the toughest to work on because they need to encompass law, technology, cybersecurity, cybercrime, and risk management. Given their complexity, if you can handle them, you can handle all other types of governance documents. If you have not tackled them yet out of fear, these sections and chapters are here to help you.

Since most of my work is in this area of cybersecurity and information governance, it is important for me to include it in this book, rather than save it for later. Most organizations need to bring principles of good management and policy work to their technology and security.

1.10 Warnings and disclaimers

We all need to make decisions and manage our own risks. Including me as a writer and you as a book reader and policy writer (we discuss risk and decision making later).

This is not legal advice nor consulting advice, it is a book to share knowledge and principles. I can only provide specific legal or consulting advice to current clients, with a signed engagement letter and a fee paid.

This book is not tailored to your individual circumstances.

You assume all risks from using this book.

I disclaim all liability regarding your use of this book.

Governance documents (policies, procedures, etc.) are important organization documents with great legal significance. They are often the first thing requested and analyzed when a lawsuit or other legal action occurs. If the other party (government or plaintiff) finds that your governance documents conflict with the law, that has significance for your organization.

I want to help you build excellent governance documents and I endeavor to give high quality guidance to the best of my ability in a reasonably priced book. But I have no liability for the documents you build.

References in this book may become outdated. Links may cease to function. Laws may change. Even when laws seem to be static, lawyers and judges may disagree about what the law is. My website may go down and disappear or content could even go behind a subscription wall.

When in doubt, seek legal counsel or other professional assistance.

I use utmost care, but I might make a mistake. Please let me know if you find any so that I can correct it in the next version and thank you for reading and letting me know. Or maybe it is an Easter Egg.

1.11 Where you can find more resources, additional reading and references

Most chapters will list some references, resources, and additional reading at the end. Sometimes footnotes will point you to them also.

With any article, book, or policy, one challenge is including the right amount of detail and arriving at the right length; not too long, not too short.

If you want more information, the end of most chapters has those references and additional reading. Often that starts with my website, which may have a page that corresponds to the chapter. That's no coincidence, since I built both the website and the book to align with my thought process and be modular.

As above, I cannot guarantee the website will stay working or freely available forever. Nor do I pretend my website is the sole resource and that I am the only expert, but it's a good start.

I will include a webpage address (universal resource locator, URL) and usually a QR code also to help you get to the main page relevant for the chapter.

QR codes found in this book will always point to a webpage within my website at JohnBandler.com.

For this chapter, I list my home page, which you can reach with this QR code.

- JohnBandler.com

QR codes

QR codes present some risk (as does everything in life) because they take you somewhere on the internet.

There may be some privacy implications also because some QR codes may provide some analytics. QR codes in this book do not provide me with any analytics and are "static".

QR codes in this book will always go to JohnBandler.com. Near the QR code you will see which page at JohnBandler.com the code will take you to. Where there is a list of webpages, the QR code goes to the top page in the list. When you first scan the QR code, your device should indicate that it is going to my website, Johnbandler.com.

In my opinion, the QR codes in this book do not present any risks.

Regarding other QR codes you may see in other places:

- A malicious QR code could point you to a malicious website, and malicious websites can do some damage to your computer, security, and privacy.
- If you scan other people's QR codes (unlike the codes in this book) there is chance they are "dynamic". They might first direct you to the QR code provider company, and they can collect some information about you including date, time, location of the scan and operating system used.

To read more about QR codes, see my article at https://johnbandler.com/qrcodes/

2

The Five Components for Policy Work

In this chapter:

- Five Components for Policy Work
- Rules in perspective
- Three Platforms to Connect for Compliance
- Mission: A Fourth Platform to align our policies to
- External guidance (that's Five)

2.1 The Five Components for Policy Work

Let's introduce Bandler's Five Components for Policy Work which we will use throughout the book. These components can be applied beyond policy work to all aspects of management since policies are merely a management tool.

The five components are:

- **Internal rules**: Policies, procedures, and more.
- **Mission and business goals and business needs**: The reason the organization exists in the first place.
- **External rules**: Laws, regulations, and other legal requirements.
- **Practice and action**: What is actually done by the organization and employees.
- **External guidance**: Best practices and helpful and relevant voluntary guides for your actions and policies.

The following diagram depicts all five components (a picture is worth a thousand words even if the picture has some words in it).

We will dive into each component in the following chapters and for now focus on how policy work and internal rules require consideration of all five. We consider that different individuals and departments may prioritize the components differently or have different opinions about what policies and management *should* be.

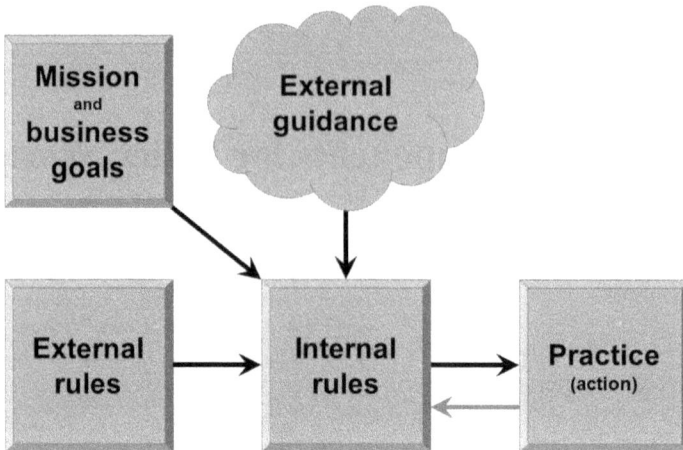

Bandler's Five Components for Policy Work

If we take shortcuts in our policy work, such as by trying to write them in a day, by blindly copying and pasting them from another source, or by using artificial intelligence (AI) tools to generate them for us, we may be overlooking some of these important components. We are also missing the opportunity to learn about and improve our own organization through the process. The journey can be as important as the destination.

2.2 Rules in perspective

Policies are rules.

"Rules" is a broad overarching term that generates different responses from people.

Most will agree that organizations (and society as a whole) need some degree of rulemaking and rule enforcement—even if we disagree on what those rules should be or how they should be enforced.

Some rules are made by government, including statutes, regulations, and court decisions. We call those "external rules" since they come from outside the organization.

Other rules are made by the organization, and include written governance documents (policies, procedures, handbooks, etc.) and less formal writings, verbal instructions, and vaguer things like culture and tone. We call those "internal rules" since they come from inside the organization.

We also experience other rules in our life. Our first rules came from our parents. Then rules come from our schools, from government, and employers. All these rules are depicted below.

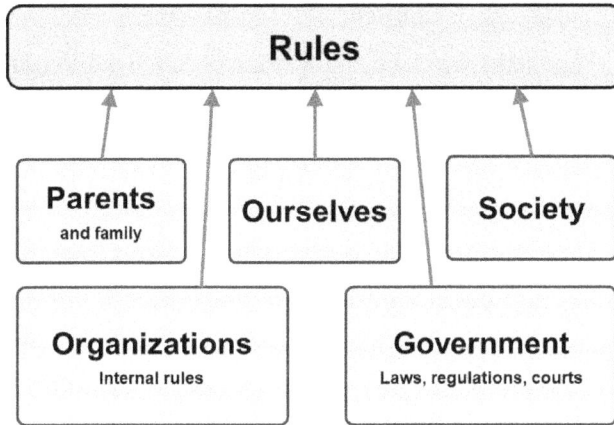

Rules

Parents
and family

Ourselves

Society

Organizations
Internal rules

Government
Laws, regulations, courts

Rules come from many places

With any rule, we consider three main things:

- Is the rule clear?
- Is the rule fair as it is written?
- Is the rule enforced consistently and fairly?

When we create policies and procedures, we create rules for the organization.

Sometimes rules can chafe or rub people the wrong way or be poorly understood. We always consider the human element and organization mission, including how we convey and enforce the rule.

With rules, we want to create them and enforce them with:

- Reasonableness
- Fairness in the written rule
- Fairness in enforcement of the rule
- Sufficient room for common sense and human decision making.

The last point is important, because when we write a rule, we are not writing computer code that a machine executes without thinking. We want the organization and employees to use appropriate common sense and decision making when deciding what to do.

Fairness and reasonableness may seem vague and they can be subjective, but are nonetheless well-established legal concepts and good touchstones for the rules we are creating.

2.3 Three Platforms to Connect for Compliance

The Five Components for Policy Work reflects an evolution of thought that began with the Three Platforms to Connect for Compliance.

I created this concept when I was new in private practice working in cybersecurity and compliance and doing policy work. I needed a way to address the "big picture" of how law, regulation, and compliance aligned with policy work and what organizations did.

The three platforms are three of our five components:

- **External rules** (laws and regulations)
- **Internal rules** (policies, procedures, etc.)
- **Practice, action** (what is actually done).

We can show these platforms with this front view:

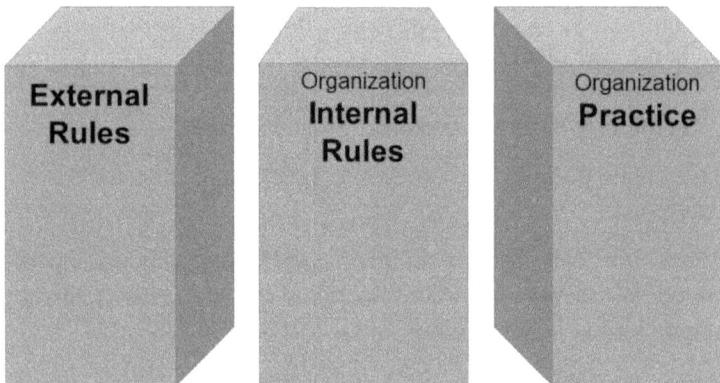

Bandler's Three Platforms to Connect for Compliance

The nice thing about this front view is we can appreciate the concept of aligning these platforms.[2] If an organization aligns all three, it is in compliance with the law. We can imagine an employee being able to safely walk across all three platforms.

---

[2] It also showcases the limits of my PowerPoint art to depict three dimensions.

The external rules are given to us (or imposed upon us) by government in the form of laws, regulations, and other legal requirements. That platform is mostly built by government and we cannot control it, but we need to understand it and its relationship to our organization.

Internal rules are built by the organization. They include governance documents, unwritten rules, instructions, and culture.[3]

The main takeaway is that organizations should build their internal rules to align with external rules, otherwise they may be out-of-compliance with the law.

Consider this type of non-compliance:

> *The law says to do X.*

> *The internal document says to do Y.*

Or imagine this more concrete example:

> *The U.S. Constitution and the New York State Criminal Procedure Law say a police officer may make an arrest only upon probable cause that the person committed a crime.*

> *The police department internal manual says an arrest may be made upon reasonable suspicion that criminal activity is afoot, or upon a solid hunch.*

This non-compliance is easy to detect and directly involves governance documents. Clearly, policies need to align properly with the laws.[4]

---

[3] "Governance documents" refers to all of the types of written rules of an organization that help govern and manage it. I might refer to them somewhat imprecisely as "policies" or "policies and procedures" and also refer to work on them as "policy work". In Chapter 3 we get into the details of different types of documents.

[4] Since I mentioned the word "detect" I want to make clear that organization goals should be to comply with the spirit and letter of the law.

It would never be a legitimate organization goal to make non-compliance harder to detect. That would move the organization into an area of willful noncompliance and deception.

The simple point is that written policies are the first things to be subpoenaed, and if they don't comply with the law, the organization failed in their compliance duty—and that failure is easy to detect.

After building and documenting internal rules comes practice, meaning action, or what actually happens in the organization. The individuals and the organization itself should act in accordance with their internal rules and in accordance with laws and regulations. All three platforms should align.

We can imagine our employees walking safely across all three platforms, the internal rules in harmony with the laws, and employee action in harmony with both other platforms. All platforms are at the same height and the gap is not too large to traverse.

Occasionally, an individual in an organization acts in a way that is inconsistent with the law and internal policy. This can be bad for the organization, for its reputation, and it can lead to legal consequences. Hopefully the organization can show that its written policies complied with the law and that there was training, supervision and other diligence. Perhaps this individual action was an anomaly and the organization was otherwise compliant.

Or consider this noncompliant organization, whose internal rules fall short of what the law requires, and their practice falls even shorter. Their three platforms might look like this, with visible deficiencies for the government regulator or plaintiff's attorney to see.

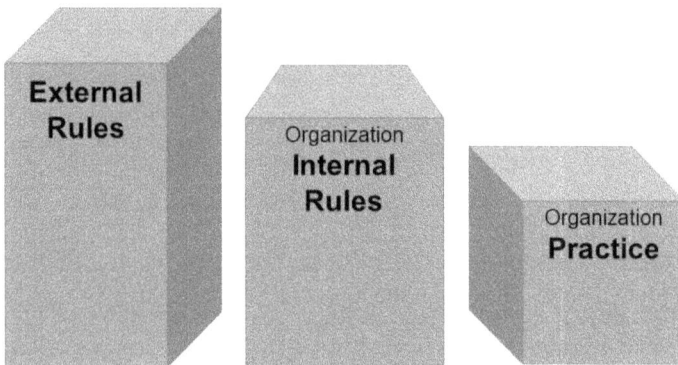

Noncompliant organization

And consider this other noncompliant organization in the next diagram. They may have "good policies on paper" but with a closer inspection the cracks, holes, and fissures in their policies become clear, and practice falls short and has its own crevasse. A structural engineer inspecting these platforms would deem them unsafe and unstable. A careful consultant, lawyer, regulator, or plaintiff would also see that both platforms need to be strengthened.

Noncompliant organization

While civil and regulatory liability is a common concern, organizations should remember that criminal liability can attach as well for more extreme cases. Organizations that actively conceal and that falsify records can find themselves facing criminal charges. Organizations whose failures result in injury or death can also face criminal charges, such as with safety related coverups in the construction industry.

These three platforms can resonate for lawyers and compliance-oriented workers, but they might fall flat for others. This is because compliance itself doesn't make the organization money—even if it might save money. Some employees are focused on revenue and other ongoing business functions. Consider that no organization exists just to comply.

Something was missing from my Three Platforms.

I needed to add "Mission".

That recognition helps ensure policy work is applicable and helpful to the entire organization, and not just something to satisfy legal requirements and regulators.

2.4 The Fourth Platform of Mission

Again, no organization exists just to comply.

Nor just to create great policies.

Organizations exist to accomplish their mission, to achieve their business goals, to meet their business needs.

In the for-profit sector, this usually means selling services or goods. They need customers and clients. They need to generate revenue. They need to provide a quality product or service to those clients. They need to earn a profit for the owners and shareholders and pay salaries and rent and ultimately sustain and grow the business.

In the non-profit sector organizations have important missions too. They may be providing goods, services, information, food or shelter. Whatever they are doing, mission comes first. They may not technically have a profit motive, but they still need to watch the bottom line, pay rent and salaries, and they need funds to come in through grants, donations, memberships or sales.

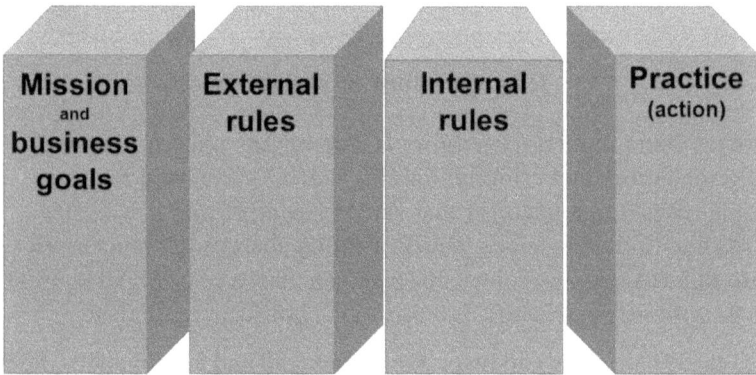

Bandler's Four Platforms to Connect

In government sectors, mission also comes first. Whether a police department, district attorney's office, court, fire department, sanitation, clerk, parks department, building inspector, military, intelligence, or whatever organization it is, they have things they need to do. Citizens and residents depend upon it.

With that in mind I added the fourth platform of Mission, and continued the concept of needing to align all platforms.

Our conceptual employee can walk across all the four platforms since they are aligned and in harmony. Employees act to achieve the mission (sell goods or serve customers) while remaining in compliance with applicable laws and internal rules.

With this fourth platform we see that every internal rule needs to consider mission to some degree. Some rules may even be focused specifically on helping organizations better achieve their mission:

- Manufacture products so the quality is excellent and costs minimized.
- Interact with potential customers through the sales process to maximize conversions.
- Manage customer inquiries, problems, and complaints.
- Securely store data and documents and find what you need quickly.
- Protect computer systems to avoid, manage, or survive an incident.

2.5 The divergence of mission and compliance and "the two lines"

On the one hand, good organizations recognize that compliance is a part of their mission and a necessary part of existing. Compliance with criminal and civil legal requirements is inseparable from the mission.

On the other hand, sometimes mission and compliance are not in perfect harmony and there is a divergence and even a tension to resolve.

Organizations can only have a single internal rules platform which they create and maintain—even if they might have multiple governance documents within that platform.

We can illustrate the tension and divergent motivations by repositioning the four platforms, instead of putting them in a line we need to move them into a T-shape. From a front view, it looks like this.

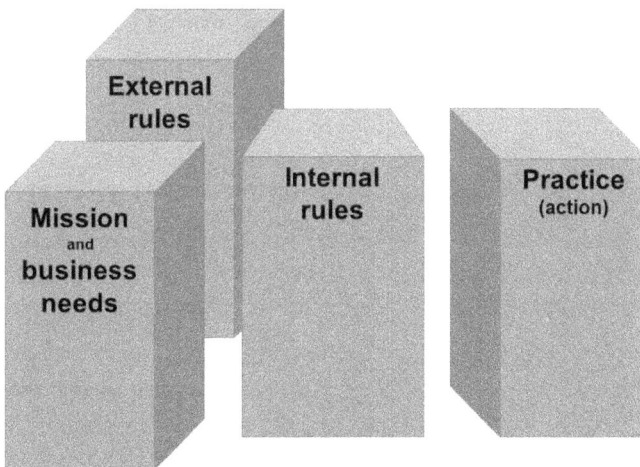

Bandler's Four Platforms to Connect (T-shape)

Then we can imagine two lines running across the top of these four platforms: one for compliance and one for mission.

Both lines run through the internal rules and practice platforms, but then diverge to either external rules or mission. This recognizes that some internal rules may be more motivated by compliance and others more motivated by achieving the mission. Compliance should be a part of the mission, but the fact is that some parts of an organization focus on revenue, others on compliance.

We can show these lines if we switch to a top view of the four platforms in their T-shape and draw both the compliance line and the mission line.

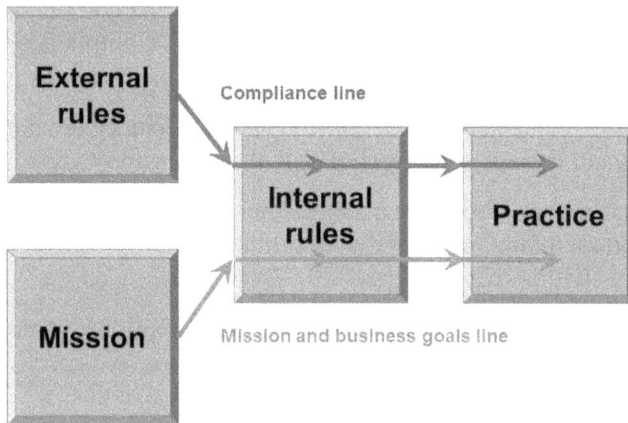

Four Platforms to Connect and Two Paths

With these four platforms the model is almost complete but one more thing was missing to build better policies and manage the business.

2.6 Add "a cloud" of guidance and now we are complete at five

To build quality governance documents the four platforms are extremely helpful but we want to look one step further. We don't want to reinvent the wheel nor operate in a vacuum and there are resources we should consult.

We call that external guidance. It comes from outside the organization, and we voluntarily choose whether to follow it, adapt it to suit our needs, or disregard it. It can include:

- A book on policies and procedures (like this book).
- A reputable website.

- A sample policy we found on a similar topic which could be adapted for our organization.
- Government resources to help understand or comply with a law.
- A cybersecurity framework (best practices).
- Lawyers and consultants.

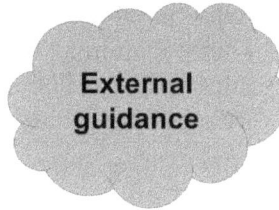

External guidance

We depict this needed guidance as a cloud because it is "out there" and seemingly infinite and amorphous for us to search and find what is helpful from it.

External guidance is the last of the five components for policy work, now fully outlined in need and purpose. We will talk more about each in the next chapters.

Now a quick preview on which components drive which.

We build our internal rules, and in doing so consider each of the five components and build and update our rules accordingly. Thus, every component feeds into internal rules.

Internal rules strongly influence action, since action should comply with them. Action also influences what the internal rules *should* be. We'll discuss in Chapter 6 how and why the arrows flow both ways between internal rules and practice.

2.7 Additional reading and references

We dive into each of the five components in the following chapters.

- Chapter 3: Internal rules
- Chapter 4: Mission
- Chapter 5: External rules
- Chapter 6: Practice and action
- Chapter 7: External guidance

For more on the concepts discussed above, you can visit:

- Five Components for Policy Work, https://johnbandler.com/five-components-for-policy-work/

- Three Platforms to Connect for Compliance,
  https://johnbandler.com/bandlers-three-platforms-to-connect/
- Fourth Platform,
  https://johnbandler.com/bandlers-fourth-platform-to-connect/
- Rules, https://johnbandler.com/rules/

3

Internal Rules

Policies, procedures,
other governance documents,
and more

In this chapter:

- Internal rules and their various names and types
- Why and what
- The legal significance of rules
- What rules should *not* be
- A rules platform beats the pyramid
- Some written words about unwritten rules
- A concept for building the internal rules platform

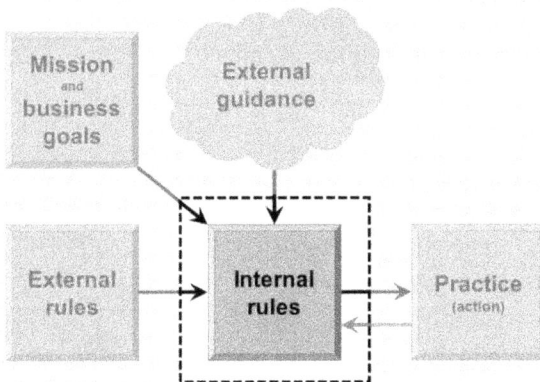

3.1 Internal rules and their names and types

Internal rules are one of the five components for policy work, and the subject of this book so we put it in the middle of the diagram and start there.

We use the platform analogy to represent our organization's internal rules. Whatever they are and in whatever form, they make up that platform and its dimensions and relative strength.

Internal rules come with many different configurations, sizes, and names. Organizations may define them differently and call them different things, so let's break them down.

The first two categories are:

- Unwritten rules
- Written rules.

Some rules are unwritten, verbal, cultural, or "understood". It is impossible to write down every single rule because that would be unrealistic and cumbersome. Further, smaller organizations do not need the same degree of documentation as large organizations.

A start-up or small business may not have a single written policy yet and that does not necessarily mean they are noncompliant, negligent, or failing to perform their due diligence. They just have not had the time (or created the time) to build written rules yet.

Eventually some rules need to be put in writing. There are a lot of different ways to write a rule, from an email, memo, detailed procedure, general policy and more.

This means the sum total of all internal rules (unwritten and written) in the platform may include:

- Culture and tone
- Verbal rules
- Policies (general rules, high level, don't need to be changed too often)
- Standards (more detailed rules)
- Procedures (highly detailed steps to accomplish a task, may need frequent update)
- Guidelines (guidance, not technically a rule, but we apply the rulemaking process to it)
- Plans
- Handbooks

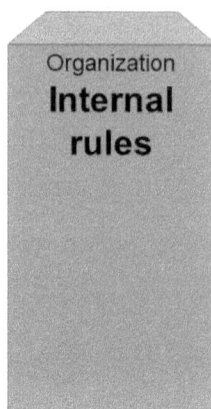

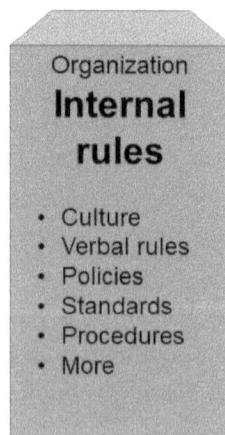

- Manuals
- Charters
- Bylaws
- Articles of organization
- Incorporation documents
- Governance documents (a general overarching term that includes many of the above)
- Signage
- More.

Organizations may use different vocabulary when writing and naming their documents. Sometimes there is a method or logic to their naming and sometimes "that's just the way we do it".

Remember that every rule requires a degree of interpretation, common-sense, and decision making. This means there is not always a clear line between what is a "rigid rule" and what is "guidance" for the employee decision-making process.

Organizations should generally proceed by presuming reasonableness, clarity, and common-sense, both for the writers and followers of the rule.

If a rule is not understood or followed consistently, then more explicit and clearer instructions can be added, including the "why".

3.2 Why we need rules and what they should be

We need internal rules because the leaders and managers need to direct the path and actions of the organization and the employees. The organization needs to be led and managed—employees cannot do whatever they want on a whim.

Employees need to know what to do. When people do not know what leadership wants them to do and how, inefficiency and confusion result.

Management can be delivered verbally and sometimes instructions need to be in writing. The bigger the organization, the greater the need for written documents to ensure the message is not lost in translation.

Organizations need to find the right balance, including the right amount of written rules with an appropriate level of detail. What is written should comply with laws, be clear, practical, and helpful. Organizations need to follow their own rules, review them, and update them periodically.

3.3 Organization rules have legal significance

An organization's rules, or lack of them, can have great legal significance.

- Policies are often the first thing requested and inspected by a regulator or plaintiff.
- Policies will be exhibits in any litigation, inspected and referenced by attorneys, witnesses, judges, and juries.

When we create or update a governance document, we impose obligations upon employees to read and follow the document. We impose obligations on the organization itself to follow and properly enforce the rule. We create a written record of organization rules. These rules and even some of the process could be discoverable in a litigation, meaning the other party would be entitled to see it.

Good governance documents help in the legal arena by:

- Aligning internal rules with external rules
- Aligning practice with external rules
- Helping to ensure overall compliance of the organization
- Showing that the organization is trying in good faith to comply and do the right thing.

Poor governance documents can harm. Some laws and regulations require the organization to have written policies. Some regulators inspect the organization's written policies.

All of this means that written policies need to in force and enforced. A policy that is "just for show" or "good on paper"—but not in reality—is not in compliance with the legal requirement. It is simply an attempt to pretend to comply.

3.4 What internal rules should *not* be

Internal rules should never be just for show, nor just to sit on a shelf ("shelf-ware").

But some organizations misguidedly do this. They equate having a document with compliance, perhaps because "let me see your policy" is often the first compliance-related question asked by a regulator or third-party. Sometimes, organizations are consciously faking compliance by putting a document in place without doing the necessary work to build it effectively and without making an effort to follow it.

Some organizations say these things perhaps without realizing the full implication:

> ✗ *"We have good policies on paper, but we don't really follow them."*

Some organizations might even say this:

> ✗ *"We need to get a policy in place today so we have it and can show [insert name]."*

Good management means thoughtfully putting policies in place with a process, following them, and continually reviewing and updating them.

3.5 The rules platform beats the rules pyramid

Some organizations have conflicting governance documents and it can be unclear which takes precedence: which should be followed and which should be changed. What is the general rule that should last a long time, what are the detailed rules which require more frequent change. Governance documents need to have a hierarchy and confusion should be avoided.

One traditional concept to show this governance document hierarchy is the rules pyramid, which can be shown like this, with policies at the top as the highest-level, and below are standards and then procedures.

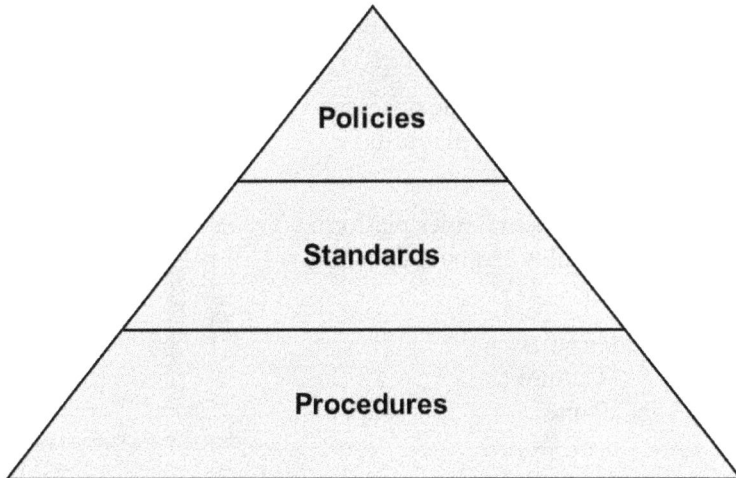

Traditional "Rules Pyramid" Concept

As recap, think of the documents this way:

- Policies: General and high level and will last the longest time
- Standards: Medium detail and medium level and cannot conflict with a policy
- Procedures: Detailed step-by-step instructions and lower level, and cannot conflict with a standard or policy, and may require more frequent changes.

I have seen the pyramid depicted with the documents in reverse order—procedures at top, policies at bottom. There's a certain logic to both options but also limitations to each.

The pyramid concept never rang true to me. The pyramid was a great shape for ancient Egyptians building a tomb out of stone but is not suited for other things. There is nowhere on top to stand! If you build it out of stone, it is hard to make repairs on the inside. If it is narrow up top, does that imply there should be less documents of that type? Which are the "foundational" documents of an organization? If a policy document is the organization's first governance document, how can we start building governance from the top as if in mid-air?

In contrast, the platform analogy works well for all policy situations. In sum, the faces of the platform are the unwritten rules which are then reinforced with written rules as pillars.

We think of our organization's internal rules as a rectangular platform.[5]

Then we can think about all the different ways we can first build that platform, repair it, and reinforce it.

Remember that the internal rules platform includes all of the rules in an organization, verbal and written:

- Unwritten rules
  - Culture
  - Tone

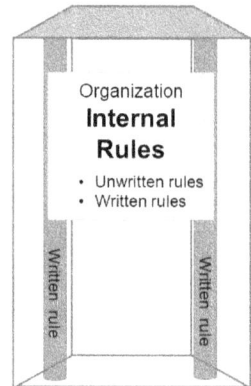

Organization
Internal Rules
- Unwritten rules
- Written rules

Written rule

Written rule

Internal Rules Platform cross section

---

[5] For geometry purists, a more accurate term for this shape in three dimensions would be a cuboid, rectangular cuboid, or rectangular parallelepiped. But "rectangle" conveys the general concept for the shape of our platform.

- o   Verbal rules and instructions
- Written rules
  - o   Policies
  - o   Standards
  - o   Procedures
  - o   More.

3.6 Some written words about unwritten rules

Consider the importance and issues surrounding verbal rules and culture and tone because they can support good business and compliance or detract from it.

Some organizations may say things like:

> *"We have great policies and procedures,*
> *they are just not written down."*

On the other hand, some laws require written policies.

And some areas eventually require written policies because:

> *"Some unwritten rules are not worth the paper they are*
> *[not] printed on."*

But not everything needs to be written down. It is impossible and impractical to try write every rule down and then manage those documents. Most organizations start with zero written rules and need to decide when to create their first document and when to create more and with what level of detail.[6]

We have some competing concepts:

- Not every rule can be written down
- Culture, tone, and verbal instructions are always important
- At some point, certain rules need to be written down.

When do those rules need to be written down?

---

[6] I have worked with a number of small organizations where the cybersecurity policy I help them implement is their first governance document ever. Cybersecurity is a topic well suited for written documentation.

Sometimes the law or external requirement requires written rules—a written policy on that topic (e.g. privacy, cybersecurity,[7] anti-discrimination, etc.).

If you are running a store or restaurant and the employee closing the business at the end of a busy shift needs to complete twenty tasks while tired and thinking of getting home, you probably need that closing procedure written down and available. Otherwise, things will be forgotten, and the same instructions must be repeated verbally many times to many employees.

3.7 Building the internal rules platform

Organizations need to build their internal rules platform. There are helpful ways to analogize this process by thinking about what each type of rule might be.

Unwritten rules are the faces of the platform

Suppose we have a small organization that is a start-up or small business with just a few employees. They don't have a single written policy or procedure, but they are well managed, diligent, and doing things the right way. We want an analogy that can show how they *could* be complying, even though they don't have a single written rule yet.

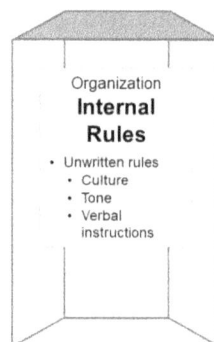

Organization
**Internal
Rules**

• Unwritten rules
  • Culture
  • Tone
  • Verbal
    instructions

Internal Rules Platform Faces – Unwritten Rules

Since unwritten and verbal rules and culture are the only rules they have so far, we can build their platform from that. We think of the unwritten rules and culture as the faces (skin) of the platform: the sides, top, and bottom. The platform will be hollow.

In a healthy organization with good competence and ethics, these faces are similar to structural steel and this platform will be solid (even if hollow).

---

[7] Cybersecurity has a degree of complexity and many individuals lack familiarity with the threats, legal requirements, and technical aspects. This is all hard to convey verbally so a written cybersecurity policy and incident response plan becomes essential for most organizations.

In a poorly run organization with poor competence and ethics and where "verbal rules" are poorly understood, given with winks, seldom followed, or there are disagreements on what was said, the platform might be flimsy as if tissue paper.[8] A compliance related investigation would reveal shoddy practices and differing recollections about what those verbal rules are. Individuals would point fingers at each other.

Your organization has unwritten rules and culture that are important and part of the face of the internal rules structure. As we write and build our written documents, we need to think about how to strengthen the exterior structure of our platform.

Policies are big support pillars

At some point we need to think about creating documents.

The first document for some organizations might be a policy—a high-level and general rule that sets the stage for other more detailed rules to be created around it.

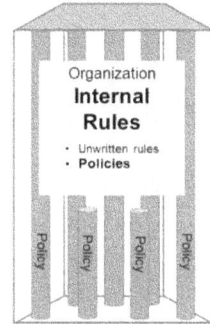

Internal Rules Platform
with written policies (general rules)

We reinforce our platform with these policies and think of them as wide columns that support our internal rules platform.

They ensure the platform does not collapse and reinforce the unwritten rules.

Standards-smaller pillars

With general policies in place, the organization can consider more detailed standards, which follow the higher-level policy while providing additional information. These columns are

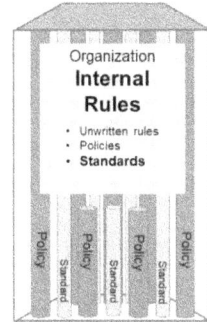

Internal Rules Platform
with written standards (more details)

---

[8] In the extreme example, consider criminal organizations and their avoidance of documenting anything. Imagine someone like Tony Soprano or another organized crime boss making a verbal statement like: "It would be a shame if something happened to that guy." Which might seem vague and open to interpretation, but under all the circumstances could be an understood instruction that translates to: "Vito, kill Jackie. Get it done this week."

Obviously, this would violate a number of external rules including criminal laws against murder. The point is culture and tone help interpret instructions.

thinner than the policies, fitting between them.

Information security standards or manufacturing standards might provide that middle level of detail between policy and procedure. Not every organization will create these standards type documents.

Procedures-the narrowest pillars

And then you can imagine procedures being added, even thinner columns with more details in them.

Procedures have the step-by-step instructions on how to complete the task. The slimmer procedure columns are nestled between the larger policy and standards columns.

For some organizations, a procedure might be the first document they create, perhaps because the owner got tired of reciting the store closing instructions hundreds of times to dozens of employees. Or because products were not manufactured properly, services not provided properly, or potential sales lost.

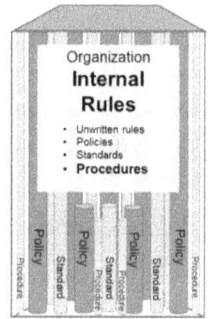

Internal Rules Platform
with written procedures
(detailed steps to perform a task)

Continuing maintenance

When we build a home or bridge it becomes an ongoing process for inspection and maintenance and the same goes for internal rules. Our platform concept allows for that. The size of the platform can be adjusted to align with new laws or changing mission. The faces and pillars can be renovated or reinforced and documents can be improved and added.

3.8 References

- Internal rules, https://johnbandler.com/internal-rules/
- Five components, https://johnbandler.com/five-components-for-policy-work/
- Three platforms to connect, https://johnbandler.com/bandlers-three-platforms-to-connect/
- Fourth platform to connect, https://johnbandler.com/bandlers-fourth-platform-to-connect/
- Rethinking the rules pyramid, https://johnbandler.com/rethinking-the-rules-pyramid/

4

Mission
Business goals and business needs

In this chapter:

- Mission comes first
- Important points
- Getting to know your organization's mission, business and culture (preview)
- Mission and cybersecurity and information assets

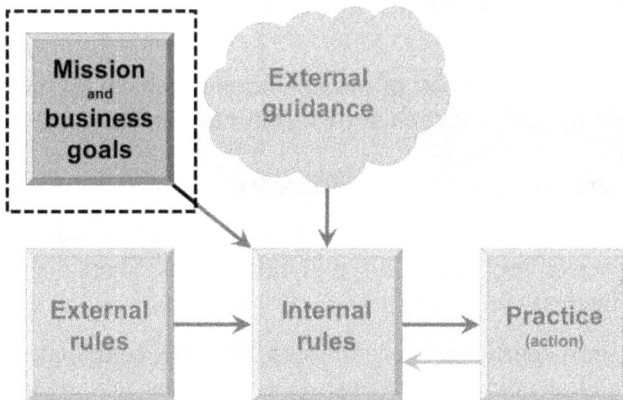

4.1 The mission comes first

Mission and business goals (business needs) are the top priority for every organization. That's why we cover mission right after internal rules (of course internal rules had to go first since that is the topic of this book).

Maybe "mission" sounds a little too militaristic for some. But many businesses incorporate that language and expressly refer to their "mission" or "mission statement".

Every organization exists for a reason—that's their mission. It might be called goals, objectives or something else, and along with it comes business needs. They may have spent years and tens of thousands of dollars crafting mission statements, goals, visions, strategies, and all types of other complex language to describe what they do. Some of that verbiage might be vague and amorphous, but it can also help to understand the organization and what it does or is supposed to do.

At the root of it, every good organization's mission is something like this:

- Do good and help individuals, businesses, and society
- Provide value with a necessary service or product
- Earn revenue and profit (which pays business owners and shareholders, employee salaries, rent, utilities, etc.)
- Obtain donations or grants (for nonprofits)
- Survive, provide livelihood
- Thrive and grow.

Remember, this book is for good organizations, those trying to better themselves and trying to do the right thing with good management and effective policies.[9]

A practical reality is that part of mission implicitly includes the fact that organizations need to ensure their own continued existence.

4.2. Not everyone sees things the same way

Undoubtedly, within every organization there are individuals with different perspectives, viewpoints, and motivations. There may be competing interests.

Some may see a conflict between mission, revenue, compliance, and security. Good planning and management principles help organizations make good decisions to best fulfill all of those important areas; to achieve the mission, protect the organization, and comply with applicable legal requirements.

---

[9] Let's face it, there are some terrible organizations in the world, some that do not accomplish any valid mission, some that should probably cease to exist, and even a few that prosecutors might call a "criminal enterprise". Hopefully none of those describe your organization! If your organization does not accomplish any valid mission, either improve it or leave it for a better place.

In a small business some people wear multiple hats. A single person needs to build business, manage cybersecurity, privacy, legal compliance, and more. For progressively larger organizations, each role may be filled by a different person or even an entire department.

While the organization is ostensibly working towards a unified goal, sometimes individual components are not working efficiently together, or might even be working to achieve separate outcomes.

No matter what, try to integrate all five components of policy work. We can create policies and practices that help us better achieve our mission, protect the organization, and comply with legal requirements. If your role is compliance oriented, make sure you consider mission *and* convey to others that you have done so.

Undoubtedly, mission is negatively impacted if the organization is poorly run, and if the organization violates the law and is subject to lawsuits or regulatory actions.

4.3 Points on mission

Here are some important points on mission, which you can use as planning points and talking points, so that others know that your policy work is mission focused.

1. Organization mission comes first.

- No organization exists just to comply, nor just to create policies (nor just to protect itself and its customers from cybercrime).
- Organizations that plan and manage effectively can better accomplish the mission.

2. To complete the mission, the organization must properly manage all important areas of the business.

- Management and leadership are key to all aspects of the business.
- Important areas of the business include how services and goods are provided, human resources, marketing (and management of information assets).
- Proper management means having solid internal rules.
- ⏭ Information systems (information technology) are a critical area of every business.

3. A well-managed business plans and makes diligent decisions after weighing the options.

- Planning is both short term and long term (tactical and strategic).
- A well-managed business considers a range of factors including mission, revenue, compliance, security, privacy, protecting itself, employees, and customers.
- A poorly managed business fails to plan and may lurch from crisis to crisis, unable to fulfill the mission or properly comply.

4. Good management generally means having good policies and procedures (internal rules).

- Internal rules let employees know what to do, help the organization fulfill the mission and comply with legal requirements.

5. To accomplish the mission, the organization must comply with applicable laws and legal requirements.

- Failure to comply with legal requirements means increased risk of legal action.
- ⏭ Good business practices require having good cybersecurity and privacy practices.

4.4 Getting to know your organization's mission, business and culture (preview)

If you are an employee of the organization and have been there a while you probably have a good handle on the mission. Even so it helps to take a few minutes to regroup, identify where the mission is articulated and analyze it.

If you are outside the organization, such as a consultant or attorney hired to work on their documentation, it is important to get to know the organization's mission and how they do their work.

Others in the organization need to understand that you are assessing and including mission, and that policy work is there to support the mission, not act against it.

Mission usually involves providing a product or a service to someone, which ultimately translates to revenue and funding, albeit sometimes indirectly.

More details on getting to know your organization's mission in the context of your policy project in Chapter 14.

4.5 Mission and cybersecurity and information assets

⏭ Skippable if your policy work does not relate to cybersecurity.

Some owners and managers are not convinced of the value of cybersecurity and the need to effectively manage their information assets.

Organizations have all kinds of resources and assets that are required to accomplish the mission and run the organization. They often overlook their "information assets" even though they are critical and no organization could do any work without them. This includes computer devices, data, applications, online accounts and networks. Organizations that manage them poorly can suffer cybercrime attacks and other roadblocks to success.

Different things motivate different people and you have seen cybersecurity marketing that tries to capitalize on fear as a motivator. Perhaps as a result some seem to tune it out. And people are people, sometimes busy, harried, and dealing with only pressing emergencies. They may think that if it hasn't happened to them yet, it won't happen to them in the future. Some even think lightening won't strike twice, it just happened so it won't happen again! Sometimes it is just unfamiliar territory that they would rather not think about.

I try to motivate clients towards effective cybersecurity and information management with a triad of reasons:

- Mission
- Protect
- Comply.

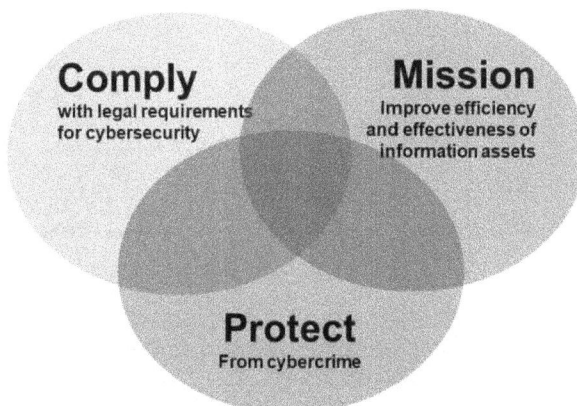

Comply
with legal requirements
for cybersecurity

Mission
Improve efficiency
and effectiveness of
information assets

Protect
From cybercrime

Bandler's Cybersecurity Philosophy

Here are reasons we need to build good cybersecurity and effectively manage information assets:

- Information assets are important for the mission. They should be managed effectively and with an appropriate level of care and priority.
- Properly managing information assets provides security, efficiency, cost reduction, and maximizes resources.
- To accomplish the mission, the organization must properly secure information assets with good cybersecurity.
- Good management principles help with effective delivery of cybersecurity, privacy, and information asset management.
- Legal requirements for information assets include cybersecurity and privacy, negligence law principles, contracts, and more.

Every organization should focus on mission, and by linking it to cybersecurity and information governance, we can appeal to that motive. As we work on protection and compliance, we better help them accomplish their mission.

In sum, mission is first, and cybersecurity and good management of information assets will always help with the mission.

4.6 References and additional reading

- Chapter 14 has a few more details on analyzing the mission of your organization for your policy project.
- Learn about your organization, review the mission statement, vision, goals, strategy, website "about" page.
- Mission, https://johnbandler.com/business-needs-and-mission/

5

External rules
Laws, regulations and other legal requirements

In this chapter:

- Why we call it "external rules"
- External rules and policies and lawyers and consultants
- Law in the U.S.—let's demystify it
- Compliance
- When to seek legal review
- Cyberlaw: cybersecurity and privacy (preview)

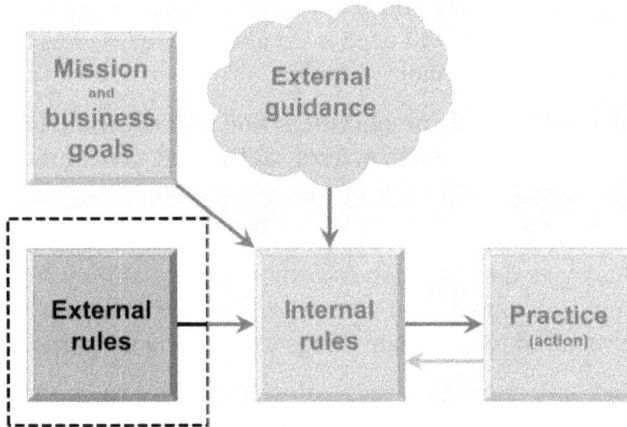

5.1 External rules means laws, regulations, and more

External rules are legal requirements such as laws and regulations that come from outside an organization. Organizations need to know what external rules apply to them, how to comply, and how to ensure that compliance integrates with their mission and business needs.

External rules are one of the Five Components for Policy Work, and part of the Three Platforms to Connect for Compliance.

Unfortunately, laws and regulations are often poorly understood and can lead to fear, uncertainty, and doubt (FUD).

External rules is a term that applies to all the rules imposed on the organization from outside. It encompasses all of those legal requirements the organization needs to think about and comply with, including:

- Statutes (federal and state, criminal and civil)
- Regulations (federal and state, primarily civil)
- Court decisions
- Negligence law (e.g., considering a duty of diligence and reasonable care)
- Contractual requirements.

By calling them "external rules" we distinguish them from the "internal rules" which the organization needs to create itself.

We should all devote some time to understand the laws and regulations our organization needs to follow.

5.2 Take charge of your understanding of external rules

When we create and update policies, we should understand which external rules the policies will need to comply with as well as the basics of what those legal requirements entail.

Lawyers (like me) can help organizations understand certain laws and ensure policies comply with them. That said, people should not abdicate their understanding of law, policies, and wording to the lawyers. Good lawyers should be able to explain basic principles and options.

Sometimes lawyers don't explain or write as clearly as they could. This can leave confusion about what the law is, what the policy means, and why we are required to do certain things for compliance purposes.

We all should have some knowledge of what external rules apply to our organization. We should also have a foundational understanding of law for our personal and professional well-being.

Sometimes we need to consult a lawyer for greater understanding or legal advice. When that lawyer provides advice, who makes the final decision? Your organization. That means the more you know, the better a decision you can make. The main takeaway is that law should not be the exclusive province of lawyers.[10]

Similarly, we may use consultants to help with polices in a specialized area and we don't want to abdicate decision making to them either.

Lawyers and consultants give advice and guide, but the organization makes the decisions.

Organizations want to be able to say things like this:

> ✓ *"The policy has that language because that is a requirement from Law A, section B, which requires XYZ. We discussed that with Lawyer C and they explained it pretty well."*

Organizations do not want to say things like:

> ✗ *"I have no idea what that language means or what the law requires, but the lawyer/consultant put it there and we paid good money for it. It's been there ever since and I don't want to change it."*

Sometimes policies are built by an attorney or consultant and it seems like there had been no discussion nor understanding about why certain language was included. It can seem like the policy was dropped in place without sufficient project work and discussion and explanation. It leaves two possibilities open:

- The language was the result of careful thought and deliberation and the result of diligent expertise, or
- The language was copied from somewhere else without any thought as to whether it should be applied to this organization.

Policy documents become a status quo with inertia and resistance to change. Take care to build them well. Be a part of the process. Do not simply pay someone else to drop them in place.

---

[10] This is not a radical idea. We should all know something about medicine and health, because that helps us take care of ourselves and our family, even if we never intend to become a doctor, nurse, or other medical professional. If we drive a car, we should know something about how that car operates and works, even if we never intend to become an auto mechanic or race car driver. This is the reason I have created many resources on law, including my online course, Introduction to Law.

This involvement ensures the best result because the organization invests not just money but also their time to work on building and updating policies and practices. The product is better and the organization is improved. They know why certain language was chosen in the first place and when it is time to adjust or update it.

5.3 Compliance

Compliance is essentially the process of following (complying with) external rules. Good organizations understand their legal obligations and do their honest best to comply.

Additionally, compliance can include the process of complying with internal rules, especially to the extent that the internal rules align with external rules.

Some organizations have specific individuals or even departments with names and duties relating to "compliance" including:

- Chief Compliance Officer
- Compliance Officer
- Compliance Department.

In many organizations individuals and departments have roles strongly tied to compliance, even if their title does not have the word "compliance" in it, and even if a separate compliance department exists to handle other compliance functions.

Titles and roles with a heavy focus on compliance include:

- Legal department
- General counsel
- Anti-money laundering (AML)
- Cybersecurity and information security
- Information technology
- Privacy
- Human resources and personnel
- Occupational safety.

All of these roles require understanding and compliance with an array of laws, regulations, and contracts.

Compliance based roles aside, the organization itself and every employee needs to comply with applicable rules, even if they are focused on other activities like revenue generation, and even if they don't have dedicated compliance personnel.

Organizations want to be able to truthfully say things like this:

✓ *"We comply with all applicable laws and regulations."*

✓ *"We have compliant policies and procedures and we follow them."*

✓ *"We have designated people in charge of compliance and other important areas, and they dedicate sufficient time to those duties."*

Organizations do *not* want to say things like this:

✗ *"We have compliant policies on paper but don't really follow them."*

✗ *"We have a compliance officer on paper, but they don't really have time to work on it."*

5.4 Introduction to law in the U.S.—Let's demystify it

Law is a system of rules from our government that establish standards of conduct, processes for resolving conflicts, and consequences when people break the rules.

Here we look briefly at law with a U.S. focus, looking at laws in our country and our legal framework. Policy writers—everyone in fact—should know something about law and our legal system.

Laws are just a type of rule that comes from government, and these laws come from different places. First, we can look at our federal (US) government and those laws, including:

- U.S. Constitution
- U.S. Statutes
- U.S. Regulations
- U.S. Court Decisions.

Then we look to state law, starting with our home state (mine is New York) but remembering there are fifty states, plus the District of Columbia and territories like Puerto Rico and Guam. Each of those also has a constitution, statutes, regulations, and court decisions. This diagram shows it in a simple fashion.

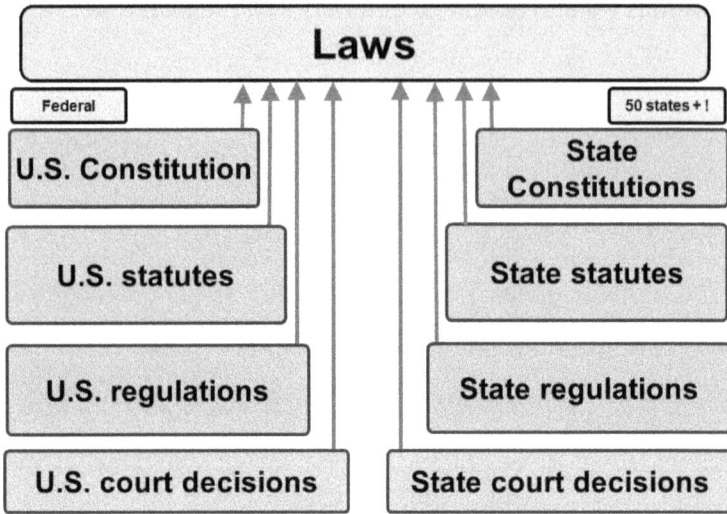

Laws in the U.S. come from many sources

The U.S. Constitution is the foundation for our system of government and a framework for all laws. State constitutions serve a similar purpose for each state.

Statutes are enacted into law by the legislature with the signature of the executive (President or Governor).

Regulations are more detailed legal requirements that are authorized by a statute and put forth by a regulator (such as a financial or health regulator).

Courts resolve legal disputes. Court decisions set forth how a particular case is decided, affecting the litigants (parties). These decisions also have broader legal weight that can apply to future cases. This principle of broader legal weight is known as "precedent", "stare decisis", "judge made law" and "common law". These court decisions have crafted the areas of negligence law and contract law.[11]

The body of negligence law is largely judge-made, and a plaintiff can recover monetary damages if they can show:

- The defendant owed a duty to the plaintiff

---

[11] Occasionally legal scholars summarize this case law in Restatements of the Law, such as for contracts, torts (civil wrongs) and product liability, and more.

- The defendant breached (failed to meet) their duty by being negligent and failing to exercise reasonable care
- The plaintiff suffered damages as a result of the defendant's negligence.

The body of contract law is also largely judge-made, and recognizes that certain agreements can be enforced in court, and if a party breaches a valid contract they can be required to pay monetary damages.

The elements of a breach of contract claim are:

- A valid contract was formed with
  - An offer
  - Acceptance
  - Consideration (something of value exchanged)
- The defendant breached the contract
- The plaintiff suffered damages as a result of the breach.

Organizations enter into contracts all the time, and those contracts impose obligations. Contracts might be with vendors, customers, clients, and business partners.

An insurance policy is a contract and assumes the organization provided truthful information to the insurer at all times, and requires the organization to notify the insurer when they learn of a potentially insurable event.

There are many areas of law (sometimes called bodies of law). Law can be very specialized and some attorneys only practice in one particular area of law. Some attorneys risk committing malpractice if they wade into areas of law they are not familiar with.

Some areas of law include:

- Cybersecurity and privacy law
- Personal injury (negligence torts, intentional torts, etc.)
- Product liability
- Employment law
- Transactional law (contracts)
- Construction law
- Real estate law
- Intellectual property law
- Immigration law
- Family law
- Financial sector laws

- Health sector laws
- Education sector laws
- Election law

And more.

The above provides a five-minute highlight of law in this country for policy writers, see the chapter's additional resources if you want to learn more.

The body of statutes, regulations, and court decisions may impose obligations upon organizations, and some of those obligations might need to be written into a policy or otherwise referred to.

Organizations should consider what their legal requirements are, and whether and how they should be incorporated into policies and practice.

5.5 When to seek legal review

On the one hand, I want to demystify law, and take some of the FUD (fear, uncertainty, and doubt) out of it, and evangelize the concept that everyone should know something about law and our legal system. Law should not be the exclusive province of lawyers. Every citizen has duties that tie into our system of government and legal system—namely to vote and serve on juries.

On the other hand, lawyers play an important role and there are times when legal advice or representation is essential. Good lawyers have years of study, training, and experience and can provide great value for a better outcome and avoid a legal disaster.

If your organization has an in-house lawyer or legal team, I strongly recommend involving them in the policy process early and often. They are already employed by the organization and know the issues and applicable laws. They probably have many responsibilities and issues to deal with, so tailor your approach accordingly. Lawyers are people too (surprising to some) and you can improve your interaction with the right approach.

If you are in an organization that does not have a lawyer in-house, this is a much tougher question, because any consultation with an external lawyer will probably cost money and because you may need the right lawyer.

Some legal services are charged by the hour, and lawyers need to make a living too. But many lawyers provide great value and do not charge for every interaction. Furthermore, law is specialized so one particular outside attorney may or may not have expertise in all required areas of the policy.

At times lawyers need more education on a policy topic. For example, some might be good at general policy work but without expertise in cybersecurity, privacy, or technology. Or they might have expertise in a certain area but their writing style may need improvement.

Sometimes lawyer writing isn't as easy to understand as we might like. We know that we need to understand our policy language and what it means. If you get legalese or something confusing from the lawyer about the policy language, some ways to phrase your questions could be:

> ✓ *Can you help me to understand more why we should make this change? That will help me explain it to the team.*

> ✓ *Can you provide me with the citation and a link to the legal requirement (statute) you are referring to?*

> ✓ *I am worried the average employee may have trouble understanding this sentence/paragraph. Can we break it up into simpler parts?*

> ✓ *Can we write this in simpler language for the audience?*

> ✓ *Can we put the more complex legal language in a footnote or in a separate document?*

All of the above polite phrases are better than something like this:

> ✗ *This seems like it was written by a lawyer in legalese. Do you think you could translate it into regular English?*

5.6 Cyberlaw and cybersecurity and privacy (preview)

> ▶▶ Skippable if your document has nothing to do with cybersecurity.

Cyberlaw, cybersecurity, and privacy are sometimes poorly understood and people can have mental blocks when it comes to technology and occasionally people start with the complexities.

We can start simple and break it down into consumable parts.

Cyberlaw may sound intriguing and new but it sits on a foundation of traditional law. We should first think about traditional legal areas that have been around for a long time, and then think about other areas of law and new laws that are specific to "cyber".

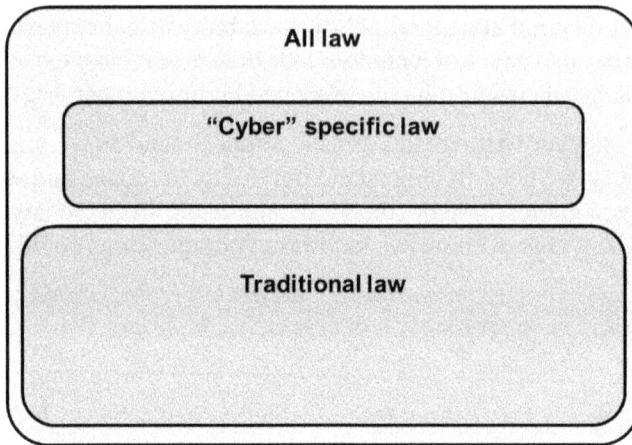

Cyberlaw sits on a foundation of traditional law

To build a little more detail into the concept, we think about what these "traditional" bodies of law are, and think of:

- Criminal law
- Contract law
- Negligence law.

Certainly, all of these areas apply in the digital realm, with cybercrime, contracts involving data, cybersecurity and cybercrime, and the concept of negligent cybersecurity.

Now we think of cyber and data specific laws, such as:

- Data disposal
- Data breach notification
- Cybersecurity
- Privacy

These laws may come from either the federal (US) government or from states. They may target certain sectors (such as health or finance) or a more general application. I depict all of that in this diagram:

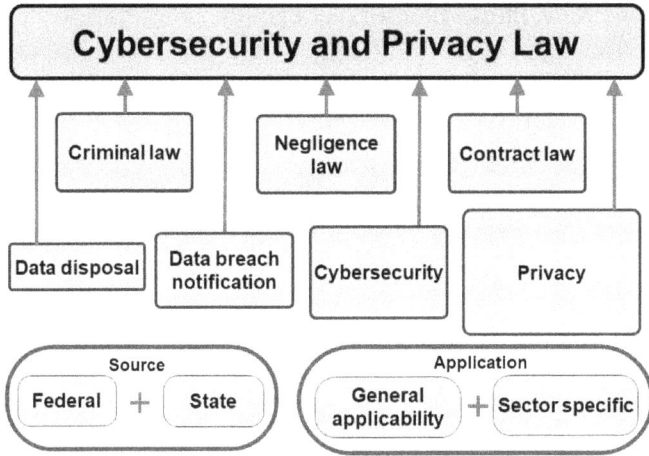

Cybersecurity and Privacy Law

Cybersecurity and privacy are growing areas of compliance that are also important for the organization's mission.

Cybercrime is an established threat that can damage our organization, economy, critical infrastructure, and result in criminal theft and use of consumer data.

Government has created laws and regulations that organizations need to understand and comply with. These laws relate to protecting certain sectors, protecting consumer data, notifying government and affected consumers of a data breach, and now a growing array of privacy law.

When I create or update a cybersecurity or privacy policy, a critical step is seeing what requirements apply to that organization and from which governmental and third-party organizations. We'll cover more details in a later chapter.

I return to the mantra of this book and for all organizations:

Be diligent and reasonable, never sloppy or negligent.

5.7 References

Chapter 19 will cover more details on cyber law.

- External rules,
  https://johnbandler.com/external-rules/
- Compliance,
  https://johnbandler.com/compliance/
- Law, https://johnbandler.com/law/

- Cyberlaw, https://johnbandler.com/cyberlaw/
- Introduction to Law Outline,
  https://johnbandler.com/introduction-to-law-outline/
- Cybersecurity laws and regulations 1,
  https://johnbandler.com/cybersecurity-laws-and-regulations-1/
- Cybersecurity laws and regulations 2,
  https://johnbandler.com/cybersecurity-laws-and-regulations-2/
- See my online course on Introduction to Law

6

Practice and Action
What organizations actually do

In this chapter:

- Practice = action = what we do
- What should it be?
- Importance of action
- When practice falls short
- Remind me again

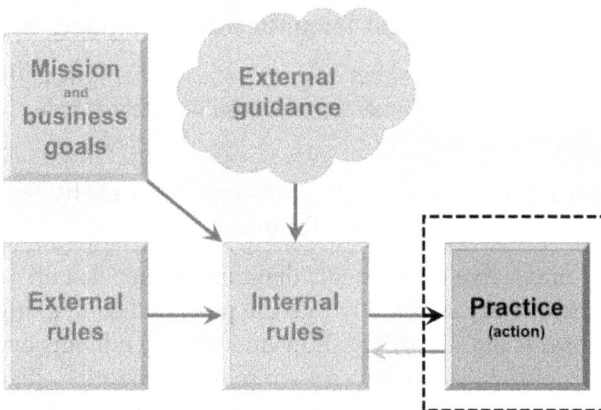

6.1 Practice and action is what we do

Practice and action are what organizations do. It is possibly the most important of the five components.[12]

---

[12] I put the external rules chapter before this because many policies are made with a legal compliance focus, law can be poorly understood, and I am a lawyer. Action remains a critical component.

Good organizations do the right thing to accomplish the mission and comply with legal requirements. It is always easier said than done.

Practice is the component where the rubber meets the road.

We can create rules and practices that help the organization do the right thing, comply with legal requirements, protect the organization (especially with good cybersecurity), and better achieve its mission.

6.2 What should the practice be?

Organization practice is the conduct of individuals and the organization in general and they should:

- Help accomplish the mission of the organization (serve customers and clients, earn revenue, etc.)
- Keep it secure from external threats (including cybercrime)
- Keep it in compliance with external rules (laws and regulations)
- Be in compliance with the organization's internal rules (policies and procedures).

6.3 How practice is different from the other components

Since action is where the rubber meets the road, it is how and where things actually get done. The entire purpose of internal rules is to properly influence action.

Remember that policies are not just for "show" but are living valid documents that are only helpful if followed.

That is why in our five components diagram, we see that all of the arrows feed indirectly or directly into the practice/action platform. The action platform is the star of the show and where all inputs eventually go. If the organization fails to perform—or performs poorly—that is a failure of practice. That failure can mean lost revenue or violation of laws and compliance issues, or both.

Practice is the only component with arrows going both ways. While the primary purpose of internal rules is to properly influence action, internal rules also need to assess and consider current practices because:

- Good current practices might need to be reinforced by written rules to ensure they continue.
- Poor current practices can be changed through written rules that instruct on proper action and prohibit improper action.

6.4 When practice falls short

Sometimes practice is not what it should be.

All of us have worked in organizations and seen inefficiencies and maybe even improper actions of some type. Even excellent organizations are not perfect and work to continually improve. There are some organizations that are chronically deficient. While there may be many reasons for failures, internal rules play an important role, directing conduct to improve action.

Problems can occur when organizations have pretend rules "on paper" but apply vastly different rules for practice. Let's be clear, a rule that is "on paper" but the leaders and members of the organization are not aware of (or blatantly disregard) is a "pretend rule".

Statements like these are both causes and symptoms of problems:

   ✘ *We have good policies on paper, but we don't really follow them.*

   ✘ *I know that's what the policy/procedure says to do, but here's how we really do it.*

   ✘ *John Doe is the security and privacy officer on paper, but doesn't really have time to deal with it, so no one is really in charge.*

   ✘ *We need to get a policy in place today so we have it and can show [insert name]. But we don't really need to follow it.*

   ✘ *I know the policy says it is currently effective, but it really doesn't go into effect until X so we can get up to speed.*

Reasonableness and common-sense remain our touchstone. Periodically a policy or procedure becomes outdated and needs a review and update. Just because there is a discrepancy between practice and policy does not necessarily mean the organization is doing something improper or unethical. Still, such a condition should not persist indefinitely.

The main takeaway is written policies need to be reviewed and updated so they align with laws and are practical. Then practice can align with the documents.

6.5 Run that by me one more time to remind me why action is really important

As we wrap this chapter, let's emphasize that practice and action is where the rubber meets the road. That is where organizations accomplish their mission (or fail) and where they comply (or fail to comply) with external rules.

The purpose of internal rules is to appropriately direct and influence practice and action.

Even though this entire book is about internal rules, remember these rules are mostly a tool to reach the ultimate goal—accomplishing the mission through action. Yes, that needs to be done while complying with legal requirements. But the point is that policies are not the goal in themselves, and compliance alone does not accomplish the mission.

This concept is a selling point for doing good policy work. We are not doing policies just as busywork, but because they are integral to our action and mission.

6.6 References

- Practice and action, https://johnbandler.com/practice-action/

7

External Guidance
Best practices

In this chapter:

- External guidance
- Where to find it
- Topics
- Tools
- Comparing guidance and rule
- Cybersecurity frameworks and guidance (preview)

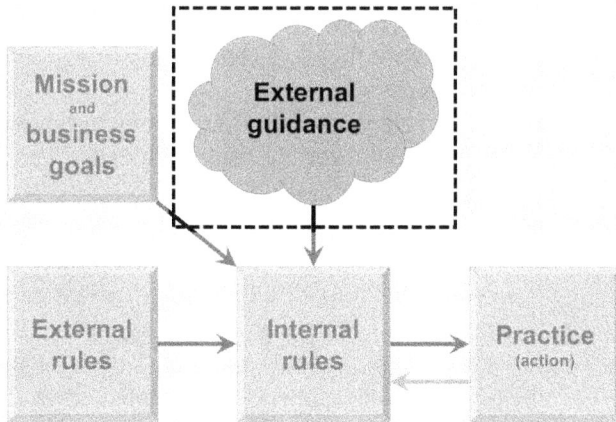

7.1 What is external guidance

External guidance consists of bodies of work, materials or advice that organizations may consult when creating and updating policies and seeking to improve their practices and action. It might be called "best practices", "industry norms" or something else.

As with everything else in policies, business, and life, reasonable people may disagree on what constitutes good external guidance, what are the "best practices", and how to adapt or follow them. Common sense, practicality, and reasonableness remain our guideposts.

7.2 Where to find guidance

External guidance is everywhere. There is an infinite supply it seems.

The challenge is finding guidance of good quality that is applicable to the organization and topic, and then adapting it as needed and incorporating it into our internal rules.

External guidance includes:

- Books (including this one)
- Websites (including mine)
- Articles
- Guidance to comply with external rules put out by government entities that regulate or enforce that area.
- Advice from lawyers, consultants, subject matter experts, and employees.
  - o Lawyers will tell you what the law is and what is needed to comply with the law. That mostly fits within the "external rule" category.
  - o When lawyers give options and explain risks and suggest a path, that may fit more in the "guidance" category.
- Guidance from other businesses, on how they would prefer you do things.
  - o Note that you may enter into contracts with other businesses that impose a legal requirement on how to function, which would be more within the external rule category.
- Tools to help you do the business of the organization (including governance and compliance tools).
- Cybersecurity and information security frameworks.
- Pretty much anything could be considered "guidance".

Guidance should be reliable and clear. Organization should be able to explain (have articulable reasons) why and how they are using or adapting particular guidance.

Simply because a webpage is a top search result does not guarantee guidance is reliable. Do not assume the sample policy, webpage, or AI generated content is reliable, accurate, or applicable.[13] Do not assume a tool or expert always knows best. Do your own due diligence and assess the reliability and credibility of your sources.

Some questions you can ask use to assess reliability, credibility, and quality include:

- Who wrote it?
- Who published it?
- When was it written/published? Any updates?
- Do the words make sense?
- Was it well written and carefully done?
- Is it internally consistent?
- Is it consistent with other authorities?
- Does it provide additional resources and references?

7.3 Topics for external guidance

Topics for external guidance include:

- Anything your organization is doing or creating a policy to manage
- Management and governance
- Policy writing resources
- General information on creating and updating internal documents
- Cybersecurity (more in a minute on that)
- Privacy
- Traditional security
- Human resources and personnel
- Accounting, bookkeeping, and tax matters
- Manufacturing
- Compliance
- Sales
- Customer relationship management.

You name a topic, there is external guidance out there somewhere.

---

[13] More on writing and artificial intelligence in Chapter 15.

7.4 Tools for policy work

There are plenty of tools and software to help organizations build and manage their policies. The point of this book is you can build and update great policies without using any tools, and if you use tools, you need to maintain control over the decision making and process.

In the industry, these tools are known as governance, risk, and compliance (GRC) tools.

GRC tools and third-party applications are external guidance. As always, organizations should not abdicate their management, decision making, and policy work to a third-party tool.

Even if you are using an application or some sort of tool to help with policies and governance and compliance, many tasks and decisions need to be made outside of the tool.

If organization management approves a policy document, it then falls to someone to ensure the tool is configured in accordance with that document. Remember that governance is by management at a specified level (Board of Directors, CEO, committee, department head, etc.) and not by the tool.

For any tool relating to policy work or governance, keys to success are research, diligence, and a realistic approach about the time and costs involved setting up and using the tool. No tool has a "magic button" that does everything for the organization—even if marketing might make it seem so.

Some factors to consider when deciding on tools includes evaluating potential costs and benefits realistically:

- Costs
  - Financial cost
  - Time to learn the tool
  - Time to input data and configure
  - Time to maintain
- Benefits
  - Saved time (after initial implementation)
  - Increased efficiency (after initial implementation)
  - Avoids organizing and tracking by spreadsheet, email, etc.
  - Shared knowledge and tracking across multiple individuals and departments

     o   Streamlines individual accountability complexities and workflows.

Tools can often help track who does what.

Individual accountability is often referred to by the initialism RACI, which stands for:

- Responsible
- Approver/accountable
- Consulted
- Informed.

My perspective on tools is that before we try to use a tool, we need to know how to do the task without a tool. For example, if you are going to rely upon a tool to create things like policy requirements or policy language, we need to know how to do it ourselves first, so we can judge whether the tool has done a good job or not.

Smaller organizations struggling with organizing their policy work should start with the basics, not look for shortcut solutions. Bigger organizations are going to need some tools but can't forget the basics.

As with other areas, we don't want to say things like this:

> ✘ *I don't know why we are doing it that way, I just know that the tool said to do it that way.*

And we want to say things like this:

> ✔ *We input X, Y, and Z into the tool, and based on that it said to do 1, 2, and 3, which is sensible because EXPLAIN.*

I have used some sophisticated tools for analyzing legal requirements for information technology and cybersecurity, spending dozens of hours evaluating their output and methodology. For all of the effort put into the tool and the high cost of the tool, it was far from perfect.

If your organization has already made a decision and is using a tool, the people operating it need to know how to use it and understand the results.

If your organization is not using a dedicated GRC tool, rest assured that all policy work can be done without them. We first reach for the tools we are already familiar with and that are available to us today:

- Our brains
- Our abilities to organize, analyze, and communicate

- Word processor (Word, Docs, Pages)
- File system (folders, file explorer, etc.)
- Other applications as needed
  - Spreadsheets (Excel, Sheets, Numbers)
  - Presentations (PowerPoint, Slides, Keynote).

In sum, start with the tools you already have at your disposal. Then evaluate the costs and benefits to use a proprietary tool with your policies and procedures. If you use a tool, always maintain control of the language and decision making. Avoid blindly following a tool or expecting it to work magic.[14]

7.5 External guidance and external rules compared

We already mentioned that any rule or guidance requires some degree of interpretation, decision making and common sense. Think of a continuum between:

- Rules that require rigid unthinking compliance
- Rules that leave room for decision making
- Guidance that guides actions.

Guidance is voluntary, not mandatory. This means organizations can seek guidance and are free to adopt, adapt, or disregard it as they see fit.

Guidance is different from external rules and legal requirements since the organization is required to comply with applicable external rules. This means if guidance conflicts with external rules, the organization needs to follow the rules.

In other words, external rules must be properly identified and complied with, while external guidance is purely optional.

Stating this more simply, the typical meanings are:

- Guidance
  - "May"
  - "Consider doing it this way."
- External rules
  - "Must"
  - "You must do these things."

---

[14] As you can imagine, I have seen tools that were misused by people and tools that failed to reach their promise.

Of course, many external rules are complicated and require some interpretation. The line between rule and guidance can be blurry, and in every regulatory battle, the government regulator will allege non-compliance while the organization's lawyer may defend by claiming compliance. A main goal is to keep your organization from getting into a compliance related litigation in the first place.

7.6 Internal guidance and internal rules compared

As we alluded to in the internal rules chapter, organizations may issue "internal guidance" in the form of verbal instructions and written "guidelines".

In one sense, those internal guidelines are not technically rules, while in another, if the organization and managers take time to issue guidance to employees, they are probably expecting them to be followed. At the very least, they are hoping the employee will use an appropriate level of decision making and common sense after reading the guidance.

Similarly, when the organization takes time to issue "rules" they have the same hope that the person reading and interpreting the rule will use good common sense and not just rigidly and unthinkingly "follow the rule".[15]

Thus, the line between "rule" and "guidance" can get blurry.

The presumption should usually be that those writing and reading rules are of good faith, reasonable, and with common-sense. And as organizations write rules or issue verbal instructions, it can chafe to constantly phrase rules as commands. When the boss asks the question:

Would you mind coming to my office a second?

They are probably nicely stating the verbal instruction of:

Come to my office now.

---

[15] Consider the children's book, Amelia Bedelia, written by Peggy Parish and illustrated by Fritz Siebel, where the new housekeeper takes all of her instructions literally. "Draw the drapes" is interpreted to do a sketch of the drapes, instead of closing them. "Dust the furniture" is interpreted to mean put dust on the furniture, instead of removing dust from it.

Consider also that some unions or union workers may "follow the rulebook" or "work-to-rule" as a form of protest or slowdown (job action). The workers may rigidly follow the rules as written for the main purpose of slowing activity.

7.7 Artificial intelligence as guidance?

With artificial intelligence (AI) tools, don't we all now have reliable external guidance at our fingertips? AI can give us the answer or write us a policy, right?

Again, I remain skeptical. As always, you need to consider the source, reliability, credibility, what it is based upon, and whether it aligns with requirements and good common sense. Remember that policy writing is not just about the result (the document) but also about the process.

Consider confidentiality and privacy about whatever you provide to the AI system or upload to it. More on this in Chapter 15 on writing.

7.8 Cybersecurity frameworks and guidance (preview)

▶▶▏ Skippable if your document has nothing to do with cybersecurity.

Cybersecurity frameworks are best practices to help organizations manage the complex activities of cybersecurity and securing the organization. They are external guidance since they are not mandatory.

There are a number of cybersecurity frameworks that are completely free and well respected, including the NIST Cybersecurity Framework (CSF). Others may be proprietary and require payment or subscription or acceptance of licensing terms. My Four Pillars of Cybersecurity is a simple and free cybersecurity framework that any organization can adopt.

The main point is that people and organizations have developed best practices in this area and some are excellent. Any best practice needs to be adapted to the organization.

See Chapter 20 for more details.

7.9 References

- External guidance, https://johnbandler.com/external-guidance/
- This entire book is "external guidance" for your consideration on how to build and update policies.
- Chapter 14 has a few details on finding guidance specific to the topic of your policy project
- Chapter 20 has more on cybersecurity guidance

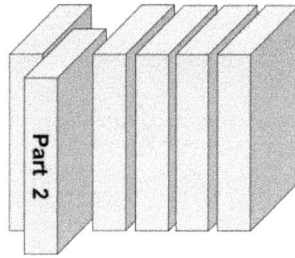

Part 2

Document project basics

In this part:

- The ideal outcome
- Project management and the document project
- Please plan for a preferable process and payoff
- Planning, shamming

In other words:

- Let's plan to build our house before we start pouring the foundation and erecting walls
- Let's check the map before we start our cross-country drive

8

The ideal governance documents and management tone

In this chapter:

- Management tone and organization culture
- People know the mission
- Compliance and protection is part of the culture
- Good business practices
- What you say is what you mean: No hidden meanings, winks or nods

8.1 The goal of the documents

Policy and procedure documents should do these things:

- Help the organization accomplish its mission
- Protect the organization
- Keep the organization in compliance with legal requirements.

Let's talk about some ways to make that happen.

8.2 Written documents do not exist in a vacuum

Governance documents are written and read in the context of management tone, organization culture, and past events. They do not exist in a vacuum.

Policy readers may have preconceived notions when they start to read the document. Hopefully they feel that management is fair, trying to do the right thing, and that the rule supports the mission and compliance. They recognize it is a rule, expect to have some discretion in how to follow it, and assume the rule will be interpreted and enforced fairly.

Sometimes employees feel that management doesn't expect anyone to read or follow the rule which perhaps exists just to show regulators, customers, or other companies. They may feel that the organization writes draconian rules to be selectively enforced.

All of this means management tone and organization culture is important. This tone can be set at the very start of employment, when the employee is given a large employee handbook and set of policies.

✖ *Scenario A* ✖

> *The supervisor or human resources person gives the new employee a short period of time to read and sign a document acknowledging having read the organization's policies and procedures. They also make a cynical remark about organization bureaucracy and paperwork.*

✓ *Scenario B* ✓

> *The supervisor or human resources person gives the new employee access to all the documentation and sufficient time (or a training program) to properly read, understand, and acknowledge the documents. They emphasize the importance of the rules, that they are continually updated, and solicit questions or feedback from the new hire to ensure understanding and since fresh eyes can find new issues.*

It is clear which scenario is preferred for effective and compliant management.

8.3 Some general principles of effective governance documents

Effective governance documents have these general (30,000 foot) attributes:

- Align with organization mission
- Comply with external rules (laws, regulations, contracts)
- Are never created for the sole purpose of "showing" to others or to pretend compliance
- Properly direct action (practice)
- Draw from and point to helpful guidance
- Establish or align with other internal governance
- Clearly written and readable
- Practical
- The right length and level of detail for each document
- The right number of documents overall
- Well organized (modular)

- Understood and followed by organization members
- Kept updated (reviewed periodically).

Some details to consider include:

- Well-named (on the title page and the filename)
- Versioning is clear
- Organization, sections, headers, table of contents (if needed)
- Appropriate time for an average reader to read it in full
- Appropriate time to find and understand a particular rule
- Clear writing that is helpful to direct or guide conduct.

More details throughout the book (after all, that's what this entire book is about) and there is a policy checklist towards the end.

8.4 Clear writing (preview)

Writing should be clear and readable. That is the paramount rule.

If writing is confusing then people need to spend additional time to figure out what it means. These are work documents, people are spending work hours to read them, we want this time used efficiently.

Clarity is different from the level of detail. Something can be "clear" without providing an infinitesimal level of detail.

The next principle is that the writing should be readable. This means that it can't always be a list of bullet statements. It also means that you must not write every rule using the word must, just to convey it is a rule. It means that you must avoid painful repetition that causes the readers to tire or mentally check out.

More on writing in Chapter 15.

8.5 ENTER: Five Steps for Governance Documents

The ideal documents exist within a process of continual review. We can think of the five steps of ENTER:

- Evaluate circumstances and five components
- Newly create or update documents
- Train
- Ensure practice follows policy
- Review and update periodically

ENTER	
E	**Evaluate** the five components of policy work (mission, external rules, external guidance, practices, existing internal rules)
N	**Newly create or update governance documents** (internal rules) so they comply with external rules, advance the mission, direct proper action, re clear and helpful
T	**Train** all organization members on the rules
E	**Ensure** practice follows policy
R	**Review and update** documentation periodically

ENTER: Five Steps for Governance Documents

8.6 People (preview)

Documents are written by people and for people. At least that's the way it should be.[16]

People set the tone and hear the tone.

We always need to consider people and the document readers. There are three main categories with respect to our governance documents:

- Writers
- Approvers
- Readers.

Writers can include anyone actually writing the document, working on the project team, or otherwise influencing the document, including the approvers. If the approver directs a change, that's like writing the change.

---

[16] Of course, with generative artificial intelligence (AI), we have computers "writing", and there are people using AI to generate content. Please don't use AI to write your policies and procedures. More in a later chapter.

Approvers can be at various levels, including the official person or group that approves a particular document, and other management authority including managers, a committee, the CEO or Executive Director, the Board, etc.

Readers include anyone who is supposed to follow those rules; end user, decision makers, government regulators, plaintiffs and their attorneys, judges overseeing a case and jurors deciding a case.

Those last few are not intended to scare you, but to remind you that these policies have legal significance and could be relevant if a legal case is ever brought. The ideal governance documents will hold up through the most rigorous review, even for the jury.

As we think about all the people involved with documents, we realize they may all have different backgrounds, education, experience, understanding, levels of reading ability, job titles, motives, and reasons they picked up a particular policy in the first place.

Any of those people could need direction and communication and could disagree or conflict with each other. Good documents should be able to maximize efficiency and reduce the conflicts and disagreement.

More on People in Chapter 12.

8.7 Additional reading and references

- ENTER: Five Steps for Governance Documents, https://johnbandler.com/enter-five-steps-for-governance-documents/

9

Project management basics

In this chapter:

- Project management basics
- Terminology
- Project cycle
- Project methodologies

9.1 Benefits of incorporating some project management principles

Whatever the size of your document project, project management principles applied appropriately can help improve the process and result. As always, good principles can be scaled up or down as suitable, and good management helps with everything, including a document project.

If you manage the document project properly, you can:

- Build the team
- Build individuals
- Build the organization
- Ensure the documents are completed properly and are of high quality
- Ensure positive results
- Ensure better compliance with the documents.

Even if you are the only person working on the document, some of these principles can help.

9.2 Projects, programs, and operations compared

Projects are a finite and limited work endeavor with a planned and defined start, end, scope, and a unique product, service or result.

This contrasts with other terms related to management and projects including:

- Operations (ongoing work and repetitive tasks)
- Programs (multiple projects with a common goal)
- Portfolios (multiple projects and programs and operations).

Projects can be managed with a high degree of formality or low degree.

If this is an annual document review and update with an established process, perhaps a few emails among the team is all that is needed before it goes for a speedy approval.

If it is a significant document of great legal or practical significance, more formality will be required; perhaps with review across multiple departments, legal review, multiple revisions, a presentation, memo, or meetings, and so on.

The takeaway is to use the proper amount of formality to improve the process and result. Don't create a bureaucratic burden or hurdle just because you see it listed as a project management step. Only impose burdens upon the project team that give sufficient return on investment.

We can all benefit from the right amount of planning and organization.

9.3 Defining the project: The SOW (Statement of Work or Scope of Work)

Depending on the document project formality, including whether it is done in-house or with external providers, there may be a statement of work or a scope of work (SOW). People have varying definitions of these terms but here is one way to think of them.

A Scope of Work is generally a subset of a Statement of Work.

A Scope of Work includes:

- Deliverables (scope)
- Timeline
- Milestones
- Reporting.

And then a Statement of Work includes:

- Project plan, timelines, cost, scope, deliverables, goals, other information
- Which also includes the Scope of Work above.

When scoping (and executing) a project, I think of these three items as the most important:

- Scope (what the work entails and level of detail)
  - Quality is a factor too
- Time (duration of project and hours)
- Cost (hours and financial).

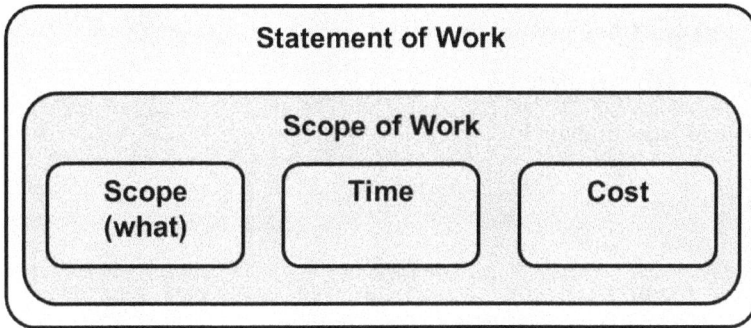

SOW: Statement of Work and Scope of Work

As the project progresses, we want to think about "scope creep". Sometimes, small changes keep getting made which can add up into big changes. If we change the scope, we need to change something regarding time or cost (or both).[17]

We want to find the right balance of flexibility to accommodate change and uncertainties that typically occur, and also properly recognize and address impermissible scope creep.

9.4 Where are we now and where do we want to go

This is where four important things need to be analyzed:

- As-is = current state
- To-be = desired future state
- Gap analysis (the difference between the two states)
- How do you get from current state to desired state?

---

[17] If a future homeowner wants to change the plans and add a new room on top of the garage, the builder is going to have to charge more money, and it might take more time. If the planned 10-page cybersecurity policy is going to become five documents and 80 pages, that will take more time (and cost if an external provider is involved).

In terms of governance documents, this means analyzing the documents you have, and deciding what you need.

Perhaps there are new laws that need to be addressed, practices that need to be reinforced or prohibited, or other improvements. We discuss more of this in later chapters.

9.5. A project has people (preview)

A project involves these types of people.

- Project manager
- Approver
- Doers
- Stakeholders.

In small organizations, one person may wear many hats, in large organizations this may be multiple departments.

As we covered in the previous chapter, documents are by people and for people, so we always consider the people angle. More on people later.

9.6. Project manager

A project manager should:

- Manage the project
- Start on time, complete on time
- Meet project objectives
- Deliver the deliverables
- Inform or consult with the stakeholders
- Build and improve the organization in the process
- Meet overarching goals to protect the organization, comply, accomplish mission
- Satisfy management (supervisor/client).

Focus on important areas of the scope of work including:

- Scope (including quality and level of detail)
- Cost
- Time.

A project manager should have interpersonal skills to build the team, get them to work together, motivate them and reduce conflict.

9.7 Project life cycle

In general, a project life cycle can include these phases:

- Initiating
- Planning
- Executing
- Monitoring and controlling
- Closing (and celebrating).

Don't get too wrapped up in pigeonholing things into these phases. Document projects can take all forms. A person might get thrust into a project at any of these stages and for them it is the "start". Keep your eye on the overarching goals.

Throughout the project, the project manager can think of small steps to keep the project going and measure those steps, including with:

- Phases, subprojects, and milestones
- Review of progress
- Updates and recaps
- Always persuading people
- Keeping appropriate focus on goals and methods.

9.8 Project management methods

There are a number of methods for project management:

- Panic and Pray (not recommended)
- Planning, shamming, when there is no time to plan (not recommended, but we have a plan for this in the next chapter)
- Waterfall (linear, sequential phases)
- Plan-Do-Check-Act (PDCA) model (Deming Cycle, Shewhart Cycle)
- PMBOK, Project Management Body of Knowledge
  - o Project Management Institute's (PMI's) Project Management Body of Knowledge
- PRINCE2 (PRojects IN Controlled Environments)
- Agile
  - o Less formal, cyclical, iterative, incremental improvement, customer value, team empowerment
  - o Our policy documents can be improved incrementally
  - o Even if increments occur on an annual basis.

9.9 Additional reading and references

- Project management,
  https://johnbandler.com/project-management/

10

I don't have time to plan
Planning, Shmanning

In this chapter:

- Planning, Shmanning: Planning when you have no time to plan
- Do no harm

10.1 Planning-Shmanning: Planning when there is no time to plan

There is usually at least some time to plan. If you have time to worry, you have time to plan!

Here we talk about a quick-and-dirty plan when you have almost no time to plan. Planning is a good thing, including with document projects.

If you are given a deadline, at least some portion of time between now and then can be used to plan, even if it is planning "on the fly".

If things snuck up on you this time, it doesn't have to become a habit. Do your best to try make it better next time.

If that annual update of the policy is due in a few days, and you just *have* to get it done, take thirty seconds now to put in a calendar item for next year so you won't repeat the emergency next time.

As you do this rapid planning think:

- Deadlines
- Timeline
- People
- What absolutely must get done
- What would be nice to get done
- Be realistic and triage
- Try to make an improvement
- Don't do anything unethical or improper (or illegal)

- Do no harm.

During this rushed process, you might need to compress some deadlines and take a few shortcuts, but some overarching principles can still be followed, including those laid out later in the book.

You might need to solicit feedback for an update on a policy, and some sample language for that could be:

> *Dear all:*
>
> *We are doing our annual update of the [NAME OF POLICY] policy and have a tight deadline. If you have any recommendations, please let us know ASAP. I know you are busy so we totally understand if you can't get right to it. We will try incorporate on a prioritized basis. If we don't get it this time, we will put it on the list for next time.*
>
> *Please give us bullet points or proposed language substitutions (no TLDR, please).*
>
> *We will circulate a draft soon.*

If the draft is ready to read and circulate, that email could be something like this:

> *Dear all:*
>
> *[As mentioned earlier] we are doing our annual update of the [NAME OF POLICY] policy and have a tight deadline. Attached is a draft revision. If you have any suggestions, corrections or comments, please let us know ASAP. We will try incorporate on a prioritized basis. If we don't get it this time, we will put it on the list for next time. I know you are busy, so we totally understand if you can't get right to it. Bullet points or proposed language substitutions please (no TLDR please).*
>
> *We will seek approval on this shortly ...*

The takeaway is that in life, emergencies and urgencies happen, requirements get imposed, and things happen. There are good ways to deal with that, and bad ways.

As always, we want to be diligent and reasonable, within our time constraints. Even if we were rushed what we do should be reasonable and defensible.

Sometimes you might need to take a stand, but always think twice about which hill you decide to die on.[18]

10.2 Do no harm (briefly)

We cover this more in the next chapter, but you are in a hurry so here is a quick mention.

Don't damage the organization with a hasty, poorly thought-out policy.

Whatever you put in place will become the internal rule, a status quo that is resistant to change.

10.3 Additional reading

Was this chapter too short?

Do you need more?

Maybe you have more time than you thought and can dig into the rest of the book, and especially these:

- Chapter 9: Project management basics
- Chapter 11: Document project planning basics
- Chapter 27: Quick start guide

---

[18] I can imagine what I might do if a client or potential client asked me to help get an important compliance program in place within a day. First, I would try to talk them out of it and convince them to be more deliberate. No good would come of it a program rushed in a day, and it could cause harm. Such a task would probably not be something I would be comfortable working on because my hasty policy work might stay in place and could reflect poorly on both me and the client.

John Bandler

11

Document project planning basics

In this chapter:

- Planning
- Scoping
- Selling and persuading throughout
- Where are we now and where do we want to go
- People and the project
- Overview of steps

11.1 Planning helps

Planning helps almost all of the time.

When a project goes poorly, a frequent reason given is that there was insufficient planning or thought, and things were just thrown together.

There is a well-worn saying of the7 P's:

Prior

Preparation (and)

Planning

Prevents

Really [19]

Poor

Performance.

---

[19] To keep this book PG rated I swapped out this particular P word.

Here's another helpful saying:

"If we fail to plan, we plan to fail."

Which is a variation of quotes attributed to Benjamin Franklin and Winston Churchill.[20]

As with everything in life, proper planning is a matter of degree. There is usually at least some time to plan, so use that time wisely, or make time. You want to find the sweet spot in between "not enough" planning and "too much" planning.

Remember that four things need to be analyzed to further our planning:

- As-is = current state
- To-be = desired future state
- Gap analysis (the difference between the two states)
- How do we get from current state to desired state?

Army training emphasized planning. First there was the set way to plan an operation: the Operations Order (OPORD) with five main topics and subcategories, designed so that leaders didn't forget the important elements especially when rushed, stressed, and sleep deprived. The OPORD could be scaled depending on whether it was for a platoon, company, battalion, brigade, division, or larger element.

The Army also taught backwards planning (also known as reverse planning and backward design). The principle is that we first figure out our ultimate mission or destination and the deadline for that. After identifying that milestone we look backwards from there to see where we need to be before that, and all the things that need to put in place.[21]

For example, if the document needs to be approved by September 1st, then the near-final draft needs to get to the approver two weeks before that, and the approver should be involved in the process before receiving the draft to avoid large last-minute changes.

As we plan, we hope it will go smoothly, taking steps forward and progressing without backtracking too much or reversing course. Ideally,

---

[20] And also my cousin, who is somewhat less famous then those two.
[21] The principle of "D-Day" also illustrates this backwards planning concept. If D-Day is the invasion date, it needs to be kept secret, or might not be decided until closer to the event. But military planners new that each day before D-day certain things needed to be in motion or in place regarding troops, training, and equipment.

we get the project completed on time with minimal stress and a process that improved all it touched.

Of course, not everything goes according to plan. Changes get imposed, people become unavailable or disagree, scope creeps, deadlines are missed. Every project involves a degree of uncertainty and requires flexibility, but nevertheless planning helps improve the process and product.

11.2 Do no harm

"Do no harm" is a physician's mantra, and it can be applied to policies as well. If policies are put in place by people who don't know what the words really say or mean, that can damage the organization.

The point of our policy work is to build good documents (or improve existing ones) and improve the organization itself. This means we need to put sufficient effort, research and thought into them.

If our work results in dense, poorly written or inaccurate documents then we damage the organization's operations, reputation and credibility. We cannot put a poor document out and hope no one will never read it—that is not a viable business or compliance practice.

Whatever you put in place will become the internal rule until modified— the status quo that is resistant to change. People are obligated to read it and follow it, and the next writers may assume it has merit and should stay as-is. Do no harm and do a good job.

11.3 Planning and scoping the document project

Planning and scoping can be a continual process which will vary by organization, project and circumstance. Some document projects need prior approval for personnel time and various costs, including third party costs. Other projects can be implemented more spontaneously. Every project involves hiccups and changes.

The overall planning process includes:

- Assess the Five Components and determine what changes are needed
  - Review mission and business goals and needs
  - Review external rules and compliance needs
  - Review external guidance
  - Review practices (good and not-so-good)
  - Review existing internal rules

- Consider available resources (budget, people, time)
- Draft a project scope
  - ○ Consider various options
  - ○ Consider taking smaller steps to avoid taking on too big a project that could stall
- Propose the project and persuade about it (evangelize or "sell it").

We want to consider available resources for the document project and be realistic. These resources include:

- Internal personnel with sufficient expertise
- Internal personnel with sufficient time to work on it (hours per week, etc.)
- Deadline (overall time)
- Budget (money) for external personnel.

We want the project to be an appropriate size (not too big, not too small).

On one hand, there are many benefits to taking small steps for continual improvement. If an organization takes regular small steps forward, the improvement adds up over time, and the disruption, costs, and backtracking can be minimized.

On the other hand, there are benefits to getting a lot done in one project, all at once. This can reduce incremental disruptions and enable large-scale transformations that otherwise would never materialize or would take too long. Sometimes an opportunity presents itself and a lot can be accomplished in a shorter time frame.

11.4 Review your existing documents ("where are we now")

Organizations should review their existing documents—their internal rules that are already in place.

This is (in theory) the easiest task and you can do it by simply reviewing and inventorying what you already have in place. In practice, some organizations are not sure what exists and where to find it. This review can take some effort but helps the organization identify its documents.

As this review is conducted consider:

- What should be updated or phased out
- Duplication and repetition
  - ○ Avoid creating duplicate or overlapping documents, and generally avoid duplicate language across documents

- Contradiction and discrepancies
- Cross reference of documents that relate to each other
- Consider governance levels of each document, which takes precedence, and who approves each type
- Quality
- Clarity
- Who created, updated, wrote and approved the documents?
- Who might have been left out of the process or unhappy with the result?
- What are the strengths and weaknesses of the documents?
- What do various stakeholders think of them?
- Existing documents may have some "precedence" or institutional inertia.

If a full inventory is conducted, these are helpful fields:

- Document names (official title, short title)
- Document type (policy, standard, procedure, etc.)
- Filename
- Description
- Comment on whether names accurately describe contents
- Dates (revision dates, approval dates).

The policy checklist in Part 6 helps for this review (and when creating and updating your documents).

In Chapter 14 we revisit this assessment of existing internal rules.

11.5 Planning how to improve

Organizations may be in one of these places regarding their documentation in general or on the particular topic at issue:

- No documents, need to create some
- A few documents, need to create more
- Some documents, need to update and improve them
- Some documents, want to throw them out and never look at them again and start over.[22]

---

[22] Of course, you won't really "throw them out" but archive them for compliance purposes and hopefully never have to revisit them. And in the future

Every organization and project has internal dynamics including:

- Which employees will need to spend time on the project, and how much of their time
- Whether funds need to be budgeted and approved
- If external attorneys or consultants need to be engaged, and if so who to choose and what budget
- Who approves all of the above within the organization.

If external consultants or attorneys are involved, that adds another dimension.

11.6 References and additional reading

- Document project management, https://johnbandler.com/document-project-management

you want to continually update your documents to keep them current and functional.

12

People

"Work is easy. It's the people that are hard."

— Anonymous

"Mission first, people always."

— U.S. Army

12.1 All the people involved

Management, life, and documents always involve people. Policies and procedures are ultimately by people and for people. Consider that people:

- Wrote the existing documents
- Will write the new documents or updates
- Approve them
- Read them
- Need to be able to follow them
- Have responsibilities to implement the policies
- May review them and judge them.

For our documents and people within the organization, we could break it into three main categories:

- Writers
- Approvers
- Readers.

Writers includes anyone writing the document, on the project team, or otherwise influencing the document (including the approvers).

Approvers can be at various levels, including the official person or group that approves a particular document, and other management authority including managers, a committee, the CEO or Executive Director, the Board, etc.

Readers includes anyone who is supposed to follow those rules including employees, managers, and leaders. It can also include government regulators, plaintiffs and their attorneys, judges overseeing a case and jurors deciding a case.

As we think about "what if" things go wrong, there are two different mindsets we can have: one is negative and cynical, and the other aligns us to a more productive and positive path.

> ✗ *No matter what we write, employees will misinterpret it, regulators will find fault with it, some attorney will sue us.*

This is a self-fulfilling prophecy that ignores the importance of the written word. Not all written words are equal and no person is perfect, but with solid effort we can have a better result. Let's reframe our thinking to something like:

> ✓ *Let's do our good faith best to write clear, compliant, and helpful documents. Most people are reasonable and government regulators are reasonable too. If this winds up in front of a judge or jury, we will have done our diligent best.*

As with anything of importance, there are consequences if things are not done properly. The ideal governance documents, backed by proper action and organization culture, will hold up through the most rigorous review, even by the jury.

As we think about all the people involved with creating and using the documents, we realize they may all have different backgrounds, education, experience, understanding, levels of reading, job titles, motives, and reasons they picked up a particular policy in the first place.

Any of those people could need direction and communication and could disagree or experience conflict.

12.2 People on the project team

Now let's think about who should be on the project team as well as others involved in the project.

There may be nuance and it can be a matter of degree as to whether they are "on the project team", or perhaps "not on the team" but otherwise informed or consulted. All of that is a matter of degree, decision, and judgment.

Finding the right people and properly utilizing them improves the final document itself, the organization's approach to the topic in general, and the individuals involved in the project.

As you consider who to involve and to what extent, here are some considerations:

If you fail to invite, inform, or consult the appropriate people, they may feel slighted and they may offer last-minute suggestions, feedback, or objections which can cause delay or require significant last-minute changes. Someone who has been included throughout the process may decide to hold their objections later since they were part of the process throughout.

If you over-invite, people may feel overburdened and not be able to participate. Choosing the wrong person could involve someone who causes disruption and conflict in the project team.

My general rule is, when in doubt:

- It is better to over-invite than under-invite.
- It is better to over-communicate than under-communicate.

As you evaluate who is on the project team, consulted, or informed, and the degree of communication, it is vital to keep relevant people in the loop throughout. You want to try to avoid last-minute changes as new people are consulted who then insist on changes in areas previously thought decided (more on approval in Chapter 17). Appropriate communication is needed throughout the project, at the right frequency, volume, and level, to the right participants.

We can think of involving people based upon titles and roles and also based upon their individual skills and expertise.

Based on titles and roles, the following people can be considered to be on the project team or otherwise involved in the project:

- Owners of organization

- Approver(s)
- Sponsor/Champion
- Workers and doers for the document (Writers, editors, etc.)
- Workers and doers for the subject matter of the document
- Reviewers (informed or consulted)
- Other stakeholders (have an interest in the outcome of a project, or actively involved in the work)
- Lines of business workers, leaders/managers
- End users and employees
- Subject matter expert (SME) (in-house or external)
- Compliance
- Legal review (in-house or external).

Based on individual skills, consider people who are:

- Good writers
- Good editors
- Good readers
- Hard workers
- Expertise in specific areas
- Good general knowledge
- Different perspective
- Understanding of the law
- Understand the organization, systems, culture, and people.

People are people. These traits are positive or might tilt you towards including them:

- Do quality helpful work
- Help you work through issues
- Help smooth through disagreements
- Like to be consulted
- Hate to be left out
- Might not do much, but won't cause a problem.

These traits might have you lean towards *not* including:

- Create more work than they do
- Do damaging actions
- Make mountains out of molehills
- Create conflict.

Every person has different motivations, and as a project manager or team member, you want to emphasize the top three which are more positive in nature:

- Doing the right thing for the organization
- Business mission, efficiency, revenue
- Compliance and preventing legal issues
- Prevent a bad thing from happening (fear)
- Personal bonus, recognition
- Desire to take on more work and retain existing responsibilities
- Desire to do less work, or avoid taking on more responsibilities.

With those last two bullets realize that the approach can influence the reaction. If someone thinks they might be losing responsibilities or an opportunity, they might react by trying to protect themselves and seize responsibilities. Conversely, if they think new duties and risks are being foisted upon them, they might resist that.

With cybersecurity and cybercrime prevention, many groups of people are impacted and their involvement should be assessed, including:

- Information technology
- Information security
- Privacy
- Compliance
- Anti-money laundering
- Legal
- Internal audit
- Lines of business, revenue
- Marketing
- Sales
- Communications.

Whatever your topic, consider the right organizational units and people.

12.3. Learn about the people in the organization and project

Learn what you can about the people who are involved in the project and their role in the organization.

Remember that governance documents do not exist in a vacuum, but in the context of the organization's history, culture, and people. Documents affect people, including their livelihood.

Documents can play a role in an ongoing turf war between individuals and departments and can create new conflict. Individuals might be wary of a document that gives them additional responsibilities without additional budget or compensation. That same individual might be equally wary if those responsibilities were given to someone else.

Do your homework. Ways to learn who is who include reviewing:

- Company website(s)
- Organization charts
- Groups, committees
- Charters for committees
- Titles
- Who the owners are
- Job descriptions
- The perception and opinions of others.

Not everything will be spelled out, so speaking to individuals is important and assessing things like:

- Informal influence or undercurrents
- Competing interests or tensions
- Rivalries
- Whether there is free and open discussion or coded language.

All of this ties into culture and tone. On the one hand, you need to understand all the people and culture to help ensure a successful document project. On the other hand, while managing the document project and building the documents, you want to try build a positive culture and experience.

12.4 People and their ethics

Good businesses are run ethically. This means the organization and the people in it make ethical decisions and establish and maintain a culture of ethics.

Ethical businesses comply with legal requirements. Compliance with legal requirements generally means complying with criminal laws and civil laws, and generally means avoiding regulatory actions.[23] Acting

---

[23] Of course, it is possible for an ethical business doing its honest best to face compliance, regulatory, or legal issues. The point is that unethical businesses are sure to face a higher degree of these issues.

honestly and forthrightly generally means no scandals and good relations with other businesses and customers and clients. Good ethics and trying to do the right thing leads to ongoing success.

Good ethics is generally good for business because most consumers value ethical businesses, want facts and truth, and don't like being deceived. Many consumers will stick with businesses they know and trust, even if it costs more. They have had enough bad experiences with deficient products or deficient service providers to know how time consuming and costly that can be. They see the value of staying with honorable businesses.

Throughout the book we have evaluated various statements or practices. Poor statements are sometimes symptoms of a problem, sometimes causes, sometimes both. Either way, we need to correct the statement and practice what we preach.

Here is a compilation of ethically questionable statements with ways to rephrase the thinking and articulation:

✗ Ethically questionable	✓ Phrased better
✗ *We can ignore this law because we probably won't get caught. Even if we do get caught, the penalties won't be too bad.*	✓ *We will follow all applicable laws and regulations*
✗ *We have good policies on paper, but we don't really follow them.*	✓ *Our written policies reflect our company position and need to be followed.*
✗ *Person X is our designated person for that on paper, but in reality, they don't have time for it.*	✓ *Designated personnel will devote sufficient reasonable time to perform designated duties, to the best of their abilities.*
✗ *We need to get a policy in place tomorrow so we have it and can show [insert name]. But we don't really need to follow it.*	✓ *We don't have a policy in place yet, but we are working on it now and will get one in place diligently soon.*

Sometimes people say things without thinking, or phrase things clumsily or poorly. That doesn't mean they are unethical or of poor intent. But other times what is said can reflect culture, tone, and ethics. Either way, our words matter, whether written or spoken, and we want to choose the right ones.

As one person asks another (or the organization) to think of ways to rephrase or reframe their thinking, it is best to assume the speaker was acting in good faith but perhaps just chose their words poorly. That is usually preferable to accusing others of being unethical (which rarely goes over well). Besides, if the person is truly unethical and deceitful, they are not going to admit it and will respond with more deceit.

Phrases like this can help suggest more appropriate language:

✓ *"I think we can phrase this better."*

✓ *"I think we can put more focus on our commitment to ethical principles."*

✓ *"I think we can put more focus on our commitment to legal compliance."*

✓ *"I am concerned this might give others the wrong impression about us."*

✓ *"I am concerned this might give others a misperception about our commitment to compliance/ethics."*

✓ *"We don't want to have a provision that puts us in violation of the law/regulation."*

As always it is a matter of degree and being understood. Sometimes the above phrases are too subtle for a particular situation or audience, and the phrasing needs to be clearer and more direct.

12.5 Internal vs. external people

At times you will need to evaluate whether and how to use internal and/or external personnel for a project. There are pros and cons to both.

Perhaps you are one of those external personnel whose livelihood is providing these services to other companies. You need to be able to justify why your external services are of good value, while realistically conveying that the organization still needs to invest time, personnel and decision making into the project.

As you evaluate, consider these factors:

Internal personnel

- Already on salary, no additional financial cost
- Already have many responsibilities, need to have sufficient time to work on the project
- Have knowledge of the organization
- Should have knowledge of the systems
- May lack an objective fresh set of eyes and used to doing it a certain way
- Assess if they have necessary expertise and skills for the project.

External personnel

- Cost money
- Takes time to procure, on-board, coordinate
- Have knowledge but will need to work with your team who has the detailed, internal knowledge
- Save considerable time of internal personnel
- Possess expertise and skills
- Have fresh eyes and are more objective
- Whatever their expertise, you should not abdicate decision making to an outside expert
  - The organization should appropriately consider and respect outside expertise and advice, but remain involved in the process.

In sum, the value of external personnel is that they have the experience and expertise, save time, and deliver a better product. Hopefully all involved (internal and external) see primary goals as developing quality documents that work and to improve the organization through the process. Noone should view the role of an outside consultant or lawyer as to drop a deliverable in place.

12.6 Advocating to people

Consider that the project needs to be sold "up" to decision makers and sold "down" to employees and the doers and others.

Whether you call it "advocating", "persuasion", "sales", "socializing" or "evangelizing", the concept is that policies and the process are important and we want to convince others of its merits so they understand the process and result, and invest their time and effort.

Persuasion and evangelizing occurs throughout the entire project. From planning, project approval and initiation, execution, and submitting the document for approval, finalizing it, and then training. We want to show the value of the project, process, and document to the team and organization.

We sell "up" to decision makers because they need to know the importance and value of the policy, underlying topic, and project. They need to approve the work hours, budget, and final document, and they set the management tone and culture.

We sell "down" to the doers because we need their input in the project to ensure a quality document and we want them to follow it when it is finalized. We want them to feel they were consulted and their input was valued, and to understand what the rules are and why they are in place.

The dynamic is different depending upon each individual's perspective and position, and whether the document project is entirely in house or with external assistance.

For example, a human resources manager or cybersecurity manager may know the organization must get appropriate documents (e.g., employee handbook or cybersecurity policy) into place and approved, but may lack the time and expertise to do it themselves. They need to convince their supervisors to authorize a budget to hire an external expert, then need approval on the selection.

Perhaps they might know the documents need to be updated, can do most of it themselves, but need to convince their supervisors that this project is a worthy priority so that time can be allocated for it. Time of the individual (to the detriment of other projects) and time from other people, potentially in other departments.

This persuasion can be done in an incremental and layered approach, so that people get regular reminders of appropriate length about what needs to be done and why. Sometimes, the reason "why" is clear to you, but not to others on the project team. A short explanation can help.

Of course, I have been trying to persuade you the reader of the merits of the methods in this book to help you build good policies through a good process. My attempts are based in facts and logic[24] and are designed to start before anyone picks up the book, through my website description,

---

[24] In my opinion, facts and logic are the most important inputs for making good decisions, but pragmatically I recognize many in our human species are not motivated by them. Still, to motivate your organization, I suggest facts and logic are the way to go.

my Amazon book description, the book jacket, and more. Throughout this book, I continue to attempt to persuade you of the merits of a solid process and product. To the extent any of that was persuasive to you, it may also be persuasive to those you need to influence.

At the simplest level, the main point is that:

Good policies and a **good policy process** help the organization:

- Achieve the **mission** (as an essential part of management)
- **Comply** with legal requirements
- **Protect** the organization.

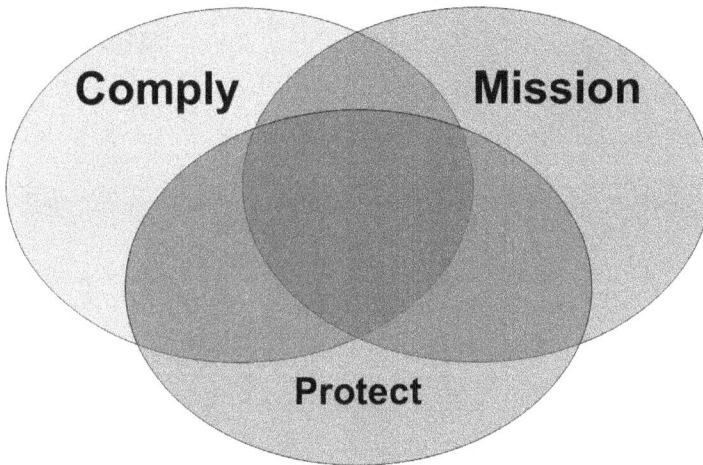

Good Policies and a Good Policy Process

Now we can layer in some more detail to each of those points:

- Good policies help us better achieve the **mission**
  - o Operate more efficiently
  - o Communicate–let people know what to do and why
  - o Manage—guide the organization to a better result
  - o Continually improve and grow
- Good policies help us better **comply**
  - o Good documentation is a first step of compliance
  - o Direct practice so it can align with policy and law
- Good policies help **protect** us
  - o Especially for security and cybersecurity
  - o Manage risks efficiently
  - o Prevent harms
  - o Prevent compliance issues.

I also have analogies we can use for our project process within Chapter 13.

12.7 References

- People, https://johnbandler.com/people/

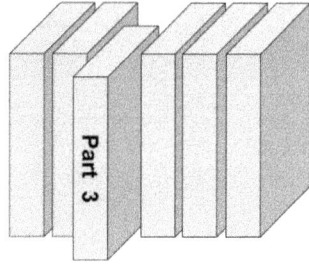

Part 3

Writing and finalizing your policies

- Let's plan our project and launch it to build or update our documents.
- We want to move the project to completion, build a quality document, and get the policy approved and finalized.
- Implement it efficiently and improve the project team and organization in the process.

John Bandler

13

Document project steps

In this chapter:

- A general overview you can adapt as needed
- Project analogies
- Review the scope
- Project kickoff
- Review existing rules
- Resolving differences of opinion

13.1 Adapt for your organization and project

Every organization and project is different. We will outline some general steps which you can adapt to your needs. You can increase or decrease the level of formality and detail as appropriate.

- If your document project is large, break it up into smaller chunks, phases, milestones or mini projects.
- If your document project is small, streamline some of the steps for efficiency.

Adapt for your personal style and the organization's culture.

- If you or the organization sometimes have trouble getting started or breaking through logjams, it might require more flexibility or spontaneity and less formalities.
- If you or the organization sometimes have trouble planning or organizing, or frequently reverse course or backtrack, it may require more structure and formality.

Consider these steps:

1. Planning
2. Approval of project
3. Start of project (initiation, or kickoff)
4. Review, assess, research and discuss
5. Identify documents to be created or updated
6. Identify each document type and what it will cover (policy/standard/procedure)
7. New documents: Create document outline (sections) and general description, perform a review cycle
8. Updating an existing document: Summarize proposed changes, perform a review cycle
9. Create first draft, perform a review cycle
10. Create second draft, review cycle
11. Other drafts if needed
12. Create near-final draft, approval cycle
13. Approval of document(s)
14. Finalize document
15. Publish (distribute), incorporate
16. Train, acknowledge
17. Continual use and review of document
18. Repeat.

We will walk through each step briefly in moment. Subsequent chapters may cover some of these steps in greater detail. Remember to remain sufficiently flexible.

If all of the above seems like too many steps, you can simplify it with the ENTER concept we discussed earlier:

- Evaluate circumstances, mission, and documents
- Newly create or update policy documents
- Train
- Ensure practice follows policy
- Review and update periodically.

13.2 Project analogies

Analogies can help you visualize, plan, and articulate your document project. Choose what is right for you and your project team. "Brick-and-mortar" analogies can help people understand basic concepts even if the underlying policy topic is complex or technology related.

The analogies are:

- A journey (walking) over a specified distance over a period of time
- Building a house
- Creating a sculpture
- Driving a car
- Securing a home or other building

Walking a specified distance

I like this because we can plan our course and where we want to go, and budget some walking each day (or week) so we get to the finish at the right time. Not everyone runs, fewer people run marathons, but we can all appreciate the analogy of walking a little bit every day to get to where we want to go. We can conceptualize milestones and interim deliverables along the way.

Depending on the people and the project size, consider various distances that they may find a suitable challenge but not overwhelming:

- o Five miles
- o A marathon (26.2 miles)
- o A hundred miles.

Building a house

I like this analogy because we can imagine the skills, tasks, and sequence that goes into building a house. We need skills, like using a hammer or saw. We need to plan, from the architectural plans and more. There is a sequence of steps, including laying a foundation, framing the walls, putting a ceiling on, approvals and inspections, until we get to painting the interior and decorating and furnishing. Throughout, there is the option to use (or misuse) tools.

Creating a sculpture out of a large block of material

I like this analogy for policy documents (and books) and the type of work we put into it at each stage.

With a granite sculpture, you start by cutting out a block the right size, then use some coarse tools and chisels to chip away to get the general shape, eventually getting to smaller chisels, rough sandpaper, fine sandpaper.

Similarly, in a document project there are some "big picture" things to deal with first, then we can turn to details with more and more precision, until the near-final draft has considered everything and is a polished piece of written work.

Driving a car

We need knowledge and skills to drive a car, and we want to do it safely and efficiently, plan our trips, travel to the required destination, get there safely, and maintain our car throughout.

We need to know what the steering wheel and pedals do, how a car accelerates and brakes, and something about friction and what makes a road surface slippery (hint, rain and snow).

We need to know the traffic laws, and know where we are going and how to get there.

Securing a house or other building

This is a cybersecurity analogy that helps when people are unfamiliar with what cybersecurity is, how we employ it, and technical basics.

We are familiar with how we secure our apartment or home, and that means closing our front door and all windows and locking them.

Yet many are not familiar with how they secure their information systems, and what the equivalent electronic doors and windows are (e.g., what "authentication" and "two factor authentication" and "access control" are). It can be complicated enough that frameworks and written policies are needed.

This is why a brick-and-mortar analogy can help.

13.3 Planning and approval of project (recap)

Consider that these projects may require prior planning and approval for organization time and budget, especially if it is for creating a brand-new policy or program.

Whether certain decisions are made during the "planning" phase or after the project commences depends on the organization and people.

13.4 Project start

The project needs a start so let's just call that the project "start" or "race start" or "walk start".

Some call it the "kickoff" but I am not a fan of that metaphor.[25]

---

[25] Here's some footnote minutiae and I'll confess at the outset I am not an avid football fan. "Kickoff" is a football term and denotes when one team kicks the

As we start the project, we want something to mark it, whether an email, conference call, or in-person meeting. Depending on what has happened before the project start, these things can be covered:

- Review project steps
- Review project scope and discuss the need to avoid scope creep
- Further research and discussion
- Research on law
- Research on business needs
- Choices on guidance
- Document types we have and need
- Document sections within each document.

The start of a project is relative for each individual who may come into the project at different points in the process.

Things that can be established at the start include:

- Start of (or continued) persuasion about the importance of the project and goals (without being annoying)
- Team building, getting buy-in, etc.
- Scope
- Deadlines
- Assigning duties (who does what)
- Communication preferences
- Brainstorming
- Phases, schedule, milestones, deliverables.

You may decide to work these tasks in as the project progresses.

13.5 Review cycles

Let's discuss what a review cycle can be and consider that there may be many of them throughout the document project.

---

ball to the other team which tries to catch the ball and run it back. There are a crunch of blocks and tackles and then the play stops and new players come onto the field. I have nothing against football (and the typical concussions) but it doesn't seem like a great analogy for an organization team activity.

We are doing the project as a team, and want to make steady progress forward together, so I like the "race start" term. But many people don't like to race (and I haven't entered a road race in many years) so "walk start" might be better. We can walk together, a few miles a day, and eventually get to our destination.

A review cycle can be formal or informal and happen at various stages of the project. They generally consist of:

- Sending information or drafts out to select people
- Review
- Feedback as appropriate
- Incorporate feedback as appropriate.

The review cycle can include:

- Circulate draft or information
- Include information for the ease of reference now and in the future, including filenames, versions, desired review, method for feedback, relevant background and continuous advocating and persuading
- Solicit feedback and indicate methods to provide it
- Indicate deadlines
- Indicate level of detail desired (chainsaw, jackhammer, chisel, file, coarse sandpaper, fine sandpaper)
- Collect and review feedback
- Respond or summarize
- Resolve differences
- Incorporate feedback as appropriate
- Prepare for another review cycle, with a higher degree of detail.

Don't be afraid of feedback. It is better to get the feedback during the project than to notice a glaring issue right before approval or after the document has been finalized. Some people might be annoyed if they were not given the opportunity to provide feedback. Learning about issues in advance gives you opportunities to improve, reconsider, or simply explain why it had to be that way.

13.6 Working through stages

As you work through the project, you will supplement your prior work (or create it for the first time) on all of those things we have discussed, including:

- The scope of the project and gap you are closing
- Continued planning and adjusting
- Review of the five components for policy work
  - Mission and business goals
  - Internal rules (existing and desired)
  - External rules and compliance needs

> o External guidance
> o Practices (good and not-so-good).

13.7 First draft review (preview)

When it is time to circulate a first draft of the policy we will perform a review cycle as indicated previously, but with a few differences.

These may include:

- Distribution of draft document with version control and annotation, method for feedback, focus, background and evangelizing.
- Feedback and edits are more general, using a chainsaw or chisel to shape (not sandpaper)
- Discussion
- Feedback deadline
- Collect feedback, integrate, and discuss
- Incorporate feedback as appropriate
- Prepare for second draft.

My version control for drafts includes annotation within the document that clearly indicates it is a draft (not approved), a revision date, and looks something like this:

> *DRAFT revised 08/08/2024 (not approved)*

Filenames should also incorporate version control, so that anyone viewing just the filename sees it is a draft and what version it is, looking something like this:

> *Cybersecurity Policy v2 rev 2024-08-08 DRAFT.docx*

These steps can save a lot of time and a lot of confusion. Confusion wastes time and can even cause legal consequences.

We dive deeper into this in Chapter 16 on managing the documents.

13.8 Subsequent draft reviews (preview)

Depending on how many changes are needed and the various inputs required, one or more additional drafts may be required.

The document manager may want to annotate certain decisions to avoid revisiting the same issue again. We will discuss writing in Chapter 15 and managing the documents and tracking changes in Chapter 16.

13.9 Near-final draft (preview)

When we are close to approval, call it a "near-final draft".

If we had a nickel for everything called "final" that wasn't really final (and was revised again) we would be rich. Many people call things "final" and label the document "final", but in our minds we should think of this famous movie line:

> *"I do not think that word means what you think it means."*
>
> *Inigo Montoya, The Princess Bride.*

In other words, don't call it "final" unless it really, truly, is final and approved. Since we rarely know if something is truly final, perhaps it is better to avoid ever calling anything "final". "Approved" is a better word that will be more precise and accurate.

A helpful technique is to include the revision date in the filename, because that revision date is a fact that always remains helpful and valid.

The document will (hopefully) eventually be "approved", so that word can be added to describe the document status when it applies. There could be changes at any time prior to approval.

Don't call it a "final draft", because that seems like a paradox: how can it be both final and a draft at the same time?

This near final draft may need to be streamlined from prior drafts, removing some comments or tracked changes. Consider making a separate list of any unresolved issues or "to-do" for next time.

Send the "near final draft" to the approver(s) for approval.

The filename can incorporate some version control, so that anyone viewing the filename sees it is a draft and what version it is, such as something like this:

> *Cybersecurity Policy v3 2024-08-08 DRAFT.docx*

Within the document can be an annotation like this:

> *DRAFT Revised 08/08/2024 (near-final submitted for approval)*

More on this in Chapters 16 and 17.

13.10 Approval phase (preview)

Now we send the "near-final draft" for approval to the approver[s]. Sometimes the approver is an individual, a committee, or other a group of people.

This near final draft can be a clean copy with minimal annotations, and with it can also be a tracked-change ("redlined") version[26] to show any changes. Of course, the approver's preferences should be accommodated, and it will depend on the organization and whether this is a brand-new policy, a major update, or a minor update.

The approver can approve or deny, and this means they also have the ability to propose or require changes before approval.

When the document is approved the date should be noted. If approval is verbal, it should be confirmed in writing, such as with an email.

More details on approval in Chapter 17.

13.11 Finalize the approved document (preview)

In sum, once we obtain approval, now we (truly) finalize the approved document.

We might incorporate any last-minute changes; we can clear tracked changes and comments and do a last proof check for formatting and spacing and pagination.

Then we do another "save as" and adjust file name to indicate it is approved and add the date.

Then we do another "save as" into PDF format.[27]

The filenames might be something like:

> *Cybersecurity Policy v5 2024-09-20 Approved.docx*
>
> *Cybersecurity Policy v5 2024-09-20 Approved.pdf*

---

[26] Word and other word processing software can track changes, and deleted text is shown with a red line through it, with a nod to the more traditional red pen that perhaps was once used. There is also usually a "compare documents" feature that does a similar process so the reviewer knows what text was added or deleted between two documents.

[27] PDF stands for portable document format and is easy to view from any computer and with any software. It is generally not editable, or at least requires special software and intention to edit.

More on this in Chapter 17.

13.12 Distribute the finalized, approved document (preview)

You have a newly approved governance document, it should not be kept secret, it needs to be distributed.

You need to distribute it to where it needs to be.

Perhaps a central repository where all employees can find it (and removing the older, obsolete, and superseded version). Perhaps notice needs to be provided to certain employees, or even training and obtaining acknowledgments of the new document.

Other documents might need to be updated to conform to this new document.

We cover more on all of this in Chapter 18.

13.13 Continuing use of the new/updated document (preview)

The documents are there to be referred to, trained upon, and used by the organization. They are not shelfware to sit there until requested by a third-party.

We cover this in Chapter 22.

13.14 Update (preview)

The documents need to be reviewed annually or as circumstances require and updated as needed.

More in Chapter 22.

13.15 References

- Future chapters have more on these project steps.

14

Analyzing what applies
to your organization

In this chapter:

- A quick walk through as you analyze the five components for
  your organization and project
- Risk management and decision making

In this chapter we step through each of the five components and consider
ways to analyze and apply the result to your organization during the
project process.

In Part One we covered each component in depth and it is there for you
to review if you need it. The following short sections give you the basics
as you work through the project.

You are not going to spend the same amount of time on each of the five
components, but it is wise not to ignore any. Whether you spend five
minutes or fifty hours on a component is a matter of prioritization and
scale depending on your policy project and overall project timeline.

14.1 Risk and risk management

Every decision—whether in policies or life in general—involves
identifying options, weighing pros and cons, making some judgments
(sometimes guesses) about the future, and then picking one of those
options.

Risk and risk management are areas that some organizations and
individuals have focused a great deal of research, developed frameworks

to categorize, manage and protect the organization.[28] You can be sure that insurance companies devote extensive resources to this. For this book, we just want to understand basic risk terminology and think about ways to help us make good decisions.

Some risk related terms to know include:

- Threat: A person or thing that can cause a harm (negative event)
- Harm: A negative event
- Magnitude of harm: The amount of the negative event
- Probability of harm: The likelihood of a harm occurring within a period of time
- Frequency of harm: The number of times the harm might occur within a period of time
- Risk: The assessment of harm and it's probability, frequency, and magnitude
- Risk mitigation: The process of reducing risks (such as by reducing harm, probability, frequency, or magnitude)
- Risk transfer: The process of transferring a risk to someone else
- Risk management: the process of assessing risk and making decisions about whether and how to mitigate, transfer, or accept risks.

People try to quantify various factors relating to risk, including with approximate number ratings or approximate financial costs. One common quantification is an oft-mentioned equation for risk, such that Risk equals the magnitude of harm times the probable frequency of harm, expressed like this:

$$Risk = Harm \times Frequency$$

There are also ways of assessing various risks qualitatively and quantitatively, assigning approximate values for a wide degree of factors.

None of this is exact because this area is complex and the future is difficult to predict. Anyone who could properly predict the future would be rich. But within the aggregate of all events, data can tell a tale. The

---

[28] Consider that NIST has developed special publication (SP) 800-37, Risk Management Framework for Information Systems and Organizations. The document is 183 pages and then there are more supplemental materials to help organizations make risk related decisions while following other documentation. *See* SP 800-37 at the NIST website, https://nvlpubs.nist.gov/nistpubs/SpecialPublications/NIST.SP.800-37r2.pdf.

insurance industry spends billions of dollars analyzing data and predicting costs. Insurance is a contract to transfer risk, where the insured pays money for an insurance policy, and the insurance company agrees to pay certain costs if certain events occur. The finance industry spends billions of dollars trying to figure out if the price of something will go up or down and acting accordingly (buy, sell, options to call or put).

In our daily lives, we make risk related decisions all the time. When we decide whether to wear a helmet while riding a bike or wear our seatbelt while riding in the car, we are (perhaps without thinking about it) evaluating the chance of negative consequences (an accident, injury, a ticket) and the inconvenience of a mitigation method (wearing the helmet or putting on the seatbelt).[29]

Every decision in life involves some risk, including choices while building policies. Policy language can often reflect a broader management decision about risk.

As we tackle the broader risk issues and the smaller decisions within the policy, we consider:

- Potential for various harms
- Probability of harms and potential frequency
- Magnitude of harms
- Whether and how to manage those risks
    - Do nothing? (Accept the risk)
    - Mitigate risk? Reduce likelihood of harm or magnitude of harm
    - Try transfer some risk? (Insurance, indemnification clauses).

Risk management is a process of decision making, and we need to apply good decision-making principles to it. As a state trooper, risk of injury

---

[29] Societal risk management decisions on these matters have changed greatly since I was a child, when there were no child safety seats and it was acceptable to ride in the back seat of a car without a seatbelt and ride a bicycle without a helmet. Statistics proved the harms that result, and reasonable safety measures are now mandated by law to reduce them. Always wear your helmet. Always wear your seatbelt. Make it a habit and we do our habits without thinking and without effort. You might as well develop good habits (not bad habits).

and concerns over use of force was always on my mind, and my decision making evolved over my eight years there.[30]

However, risk is often focused on harms, not potential benefits. Decision making needs to weigh both, and we discuss that next.

14.2 Decision making

Policy writing, risk management, and all aspects of life require good decision making. This requires accurate information (facts), logic, and a reasonable logical process.

In sum, identify valid options, weigh the potential pros and cons of each (including likelihoods and magnitudes of the pros and cons), and discuss and arrive at a reasonable decision you can justify.

Consider these principles to ease decision making.

1. Identify relevant, accurate facts and information
2. Apply logic, reason, and common sense
3. Try to break bigger decisions into smaller parts
4. Try to identify what decisions are independent of others, and which are connected to others.
5. Where two or more decisions are connected to each other, try isolate and identify what the connections are and what effects they have
6. Try to identify which decisions need to come first ("threshold issues")
7. When you have isolated a decision point, identify options
    a. When you are identifying options, it helps to identify obvious options, extreme options, and terrible options

---

[30] As a state trooper, I needed to prioritize risks with the goal of not being seriously injured or killed during my shift. While my station provided full-service policing one occasional duty was highway traffic enforcement. One risk was stopping a car that could possibly have a wanted felon inside who was willing to shoot me. Another risk was being hit by an inattentive motorist while I stood on the side of the road. After a few close calls, I came to realize that the chance of being shot by the motorist I just pulled over was very slim, maybe one in a million. However, the chance of me being struck by a passing motorist or truck was much higher, maybe one in ten thousand. My actions evolved to quickly assess the vehicle occupants and then pay a higher degree of attention to passing vehicles. Other actions evolved over the years as well based on my perception of various risks.

  b. Extreme and terrible options are helpful to identify because they show that more reasonable options are more workable. The only danger of specifying extreme and terrible options is if your group has an unreasonable person who might seize upon the extreme terrible option thinking it is a good one.

  c. Don't spend too much time identifying too many extreme and terrible options.

8. After you identify all the options, identify the pros (potential benefits) and cons (risks and potential harms) of each, using common sense and risk analysis.

  a. Risk analysis means evaluating the potential harms and magnitudes of those harms. Take comfort that predicting the future is hard and approximate.

  b. Don't forget to evaluate the potential benefits of each option. As above, predicting the future is hard.

  c. Rule out the extreme and terrible options. That should be easy.

  d. Evaluate the remaining options with greater detail and discussion.

9. Good decision-making means evaluating all the factors and making a reasonable choice.

10. Consider the "business judgment rule", a legal concept that indicates decisions should be made in good faith, with reasonable care, acting in the best interests of the organization.[31]

11. Solicit necessary feedback, inform and consult as needed

12. Consider who needs to approve the decision

13. If needed, make recommendation for the decision to the approver, stating reasons for the proposed decision.

As you consider decisions, and which are "yours" to make, and which belong to people higher in the organization, consider that you will always need to be able to justify your actions and decisions. If a decision is for someone above you, be sure to present them with valid options and a helpful framework to assist in their decision, including by making your recommendation and reasons why.

---

[31] Generally, it means doing ones best to make the right decision for the right reason, recognizing that not every decision works out perfectly in the end. More technically, it is a shield from certain liability when decisions are made in an appropriate manner. *See,*
https://www.law.cornell.edu/wex/business_judgment_rule

There are often going to be multiple options and disagreements, so we dive into resolving differences of opinion in Chapter 16.

14.3 Mission analysis

Mission is the first of the five components to analyze for the document project. We discussed Mission in Chapter 4.[32]

Since every organization exists to achieve a mission (and not just to create policies or comply with regulations) and since policies can help achieve and support the mission, we always want to keep our eye on this component.

We can identify organization mission, business goals, and business needs in various places and mediums, including:

- Website (including "about" page)
- Mission statement
- Programs, products, services
- Annual reports and filings
- People.

Mission is usually tied to revenue or funding, so evaluate where the organization gets the funds it needs to operate. Consider the proportion of funds from each source because that affects how to prioritize each. Also consider future plans and whether certain revenue sources or lines of business will be increased or decreased.

Mission may have a different flavor depending on whether the organization is for profit, non-profit, or governmental, and based on type

---

[32] Readers might wonder why the internal rules Chapter 3 preceded the mission Chapter 4 while here the mission section comes first. Here is my thinking:
 You are reading this book to help with policies and procedures (internal rules) and we needed to set a foundation about what internal rules are and should be, so we covered internal rules first in the book.
 But now you are working on the project and you probably know a bit about the organization's mission. Mission comes first so you can assess this first and possibly very quickly. Then you will be able to assure stakeholders and approvers that your policy project addresses mission, and then move on to address other important components, including compliance and practice.

of organization and sector. Rest assured that every organization has some type of mission or business goals to consider.[33]

If the policy project is compliance motivated or focused, you may be able to assess mission relatively quickly and move on. But don't ignore mission, and ensure everyone knows policies are there to support the mission, not hinder it.

14.4 Internal rules analysis (existing and desired)

This is the heart of your policy project and this entire book.

In sum you will analyze:

- What are your existing internal rules?
- What are your desired internal rules?
- What changes should you (or will you) make? (the gap you are closing).

Internal rules include:

- Articles of incorporation
- Bylaws
- Policies
- Standards
- Procedures
- Handbooks
- Etc.

Chapter 3 and the policy checklist in Part 5 have more on this.

14.5 External rules analysis

Many policy projects have a compliance motivation and focus, and we dedicated Chapter 5 to addressing laws and regulations and other legal requirements.[34]

We dive into cybersecurity laws in Chapter 19.

---

[33] If your organization truly has no mission, or if sufficient people in your organization believe it has no mission, it is probably time to find another organization.

[34] As we covered, even if the policy is compliance motivated, no organization exists just to comply, so this is why we also consider mission as a key component.

For your organization you will analyze:

- What are the external rules that apply to the organization? (starting with the highest priority rules)
- External rules include:
  - Laws and regulations
  - Criminal laws
  - Code requirements (e.g., building code, etc.)
  - Negligence law (e.g. be diligent and reasonable)
  - Contracts (with customers, clients, business partners, and insurance policies)
- Who enforces those external rules and how?
- Do our policies point to those external rules?
- Have we consulted with legal counsel on this recently?
  - Do we need to consult or refresh that consultation with legal counsel?

14.6 Practice analysis (existing and desired)

We devoted Chapter 6 to practice and action.

In sum we will examine:

- What good existing practices should be reinforced in a written internal rule?
- What bad practices should be corrected by specifying the proper action?
- What bad practices should be corrected by specifically prohibiting them in a written rule?

Where practices are deficient and need correction, there can be value in a certain amount of redundancy to avoid doubt and correct behavior. For example:

- State how we should operate
- State and prohibit improper methods and operations
- State *why* the proper methods should be followed (if people understand why, they are more likely to remember and practice the correct way to do it).

Quality employees who are doing the job are excellent sources of information about what is being done and what should be done.

14.7 External guidance analysis

In sum, you will analyze:

- Writings and guidance from the particular government agency that enforces important external rules regarding your organization
  - General guidance provided to help understand the spirit of the law/regulation
  - Details helpful for policy and practice
    - Deadlines
    - Filings
    - Technical requirements
    - Spelling out important issues in the law/regulation
    - Clarifying general info
    - Clarifying confusing information in the law/regulation
- What external guidance is currently used by the organization
  - Best practices and frameworks
  - Outside experts, lawyers, consultants
  - Tools
  - Reliability and credibility
  - How it has been adapted for the organization
  - Costs, risks, and benefits of the external guidance
- Should we perform additional research to find more external guidance?
  - Industry groups that provide helpful external guidance
  - Evaluate other criteria as above
- Would outside expertise in this topic area be helpful?
  - Subject matter expertise or consultants
  - Legal counsel.

We dedicated Chapter 7 to external guidance and Chapter 20 to cybersecurity guidance.

14.8 Additional reading and references

We provided references with each section, here is a consolidated list.

- Risk, https://johnbandler.com/risk/
- Internal rules, Chapter 3 (and the rest of this book)
- Mission, Chapter 4

- External rules, Chapter 5
- External rules for cybersecurity, Chapter 19
- Practice and action, Chapter 6
- External guidance, Chapter 7
- External guidance for cybersecurity, Chapter 20

15

Writing

In this chapter:

- Reading, writing, technical writing, editing
- Rithmatic too (just a little)

15.1 We can improve our writing

Writing is an important personal and professional skill. The most important point to take away is that you *can* improve your writing skills, no matter where you are now, no matter what your native language, background, or education.

Let's first acknowledge that many people dislike writing, are fearful about it, and lack confidence. If that is you, keep reading and keep practicing.

Let's also acknowledge that I do not pretend to be a writing expert. Still, I have a bit of experience and practice with it, and I have come a long way over the years.[35]

---

[35] I have struggled with papers, documents and more just like every person. Over the years I have written a lot. High school and college papers. Then as a Trooper I typed hundreds of arrest and investigation report narratives. Law school writing and as a prosecutor I drafted complaints, indictments, search warrants, motions, letters and more letters. After leaving government, I have written books, articles, courses, etc. and had dozens of people offering feedback—I still have them in my mind as I write.

As an adjunct professor I have taught hundreds of students and read thousands of written submissions which has given me additional insight into how people write and learn.

Whatever the writing style and quality of this book, and I tried my best. It is not perfect but it is a lot better than what I would have written years ago! Writing improvement—not perfection—is the key of this section.

Here are some facts about each of us as individuals:

- Practice and effort help us improve
- No matter the quality of your writing right now, you can improve
- No matter how much you might not enjoy writing …
    - You can gain an appreciation for it
    - It will become easier
    - You might even grow to like it
    - You might grow to excel at it.

If your governance documents are written well, they can:

- Best achieve the goals of the document
- Avoid confusion
- Save time.

15.2 Writing skills

Writing takes a lot of different skills including these basic skills:

- Typing
- Word-processing.

The first skill that will help you is knowing how to type. If you cannot type yet make it a point to learn. Be able to touch type; by feel, without looking at the keyboard. There are many free apps and online sites to help you with this. Investing a little time each day will make a significant difference.[36]

Another skill that will help you vastly is word processing. There are many options including Microsoft Word, Google's Docs, Apple's Pages, or other tools for writing, formatting, editing, and managing documents. Do not rest on your laurels and keep exploring the features of the applications and the way you are managing your documents.[37]

---

[36] Once upon a time I did not know how to type well, and this hampered my work in my first job out of college at a small software company. I learned to type well, and it improved my work. Then I became a Trooper and when there was a large arrest someone was needed to do the typing and I gladly took that assignment. It suited me fine, since it meant someone else got the coffee, our meal, did the fingerprinting and photographing, or whatever else was needed as I sat at the computer and typed away on arrest reports and criminal complaints.
[37] Working on this book has been a learning process for me as well, as I have dived deep into formatting, styles, sections, and more.

15.3 Writing components

Policies and documents are made up of components, just like our conceptual internal rules platform, a wall, or a house.

Like building a house, it is important to first come up with a plan of what it will look like and how it will be structured. That could be an outline, which can eventually become the table of contents (if needed).[38]

The components of our governance documents include these elements:

- Title
- Table of contents/outline
- Document
    - Sections (including revision history, etcetera)
    - Paragraphs
    - Sentences
    - Words
    - Letters, punctuation.

Early outline and planning and size

As you plan and start to work on the document, early steps include creating these elements:

- Title of document (may evolve, so consider options)
- Relationship of this document to other governance documents
- Outline (of initial draft, which may shift as work progresses)
    - Introduction
    - Each section
    - Figure out what belongs in this document or should go in another
    - Conclusion
    - Total word count (desired, actual)
    - Percentage or word count spent on each section.

Size matters and there are always more than the two choices "all or nothing". We are trying to create efficient, practical governance documents. If we are creating a written rule for our organization, we need to decide whether that rule should be in one sentence, one

---

[38] Outlines are important even if some people do not like to do them. I have even had law students tell me they have never done an outline in their life (which makes me wonder about their college education). Remember that outlines are a planning tool and outlines can evolve with the document.

paragraph, a page, section, entire document, or suite of documents the size of a book. It is helpful to have an approximate word budget in mind. More on word count later.

Again, never succumb to the fallacy that a topic requires either massive detail or nothing at all. You have the full continuum to choose from, from nothing, to a single sentence, and any size appropriate.

15.4 Word choice

Word choice is important to accurately convey meaning to the reader.

Normally, consistency with word choice is helpful so that everyone knows what you mean every time you use that same word. Varying the word can make the reader think it is a different thing or concept you are talking about.

That said, occasionally, repeating the same word can be tiring and the reader needs some variety. Using a thesaurus and finding synonyms can help.

The writer should always know the meaning of words they use. This sounds simple, but many make this mistake. Know your audience and the circumstances under which they will use the documents. Your job is to write clearly, not impress anyone with fancy vocabulary.

Writers should be aware that a single word (or phrase) can mean different things to different people. If that confusion is going to exist, look for ways to be clear.

Try not to alienate or offend the audience. Proper word choice and phrasing can help with that.

Comply with organization rules and norms with word choice.

15.5 Sentences

Write directly and use an active voice. It is preferred to avoid writing something with a passive voice (see what I just did there?). Be direct and say what you want to say. Try to avoid complex sentences that take the reader around a bush until finally arriving at your conclusion or main point.

While it is helpful to vary sentence length to keep the reader engaged, if you are crafting difficult governance language or rules, it often helps to keep the sentences simple, with one point per sentence.

This is especially important when you are working to identify and resolve differences of opinion.

Remember that your goal is clarity and efficiency. Write for your audience so that they understand and do not try to impress readers with the complexity of your sentence structure.[39] Now that I have emphasized the importance of crisp, clear sentences, realize that in some situations variety is helpful, and consider this footnote.[40]

15.6 Paragraphs

Lead with the most important point of the paragraph. Make your first sentence your topic sentence. Don't make the reader wade through the entire paragraph to find it or figure it out. Don't bury the topic of the paragraph or beat around the bush to arrive at a stunning conclusion or reversal late in the paragraph.[41] A busy or lazy reader might not get past the first sentence. Limit your topics to one per paragraph.

---

[39] Alas, some lawyers seem to have come out of law school writing worse than they went in. Especially in law, a goal should be clear writing, with limited legalese and legalism. Facts need to be outlined, law needs to be summarized, and people need to be persuaded. Litigants and judges alike should strive for clarity. We want to convey our point, not impress others with our intellect.

[40] We are writing policies, not a bestselling novel nor a Shakespearian play so our main goal is clarity, accuracy, and readability. But while we are on the topic of sentence length, consider this paragraph by the late Gary Provost, a noted writing teacher:

> *"This sentence has five words. Here are five more words. Five-word sentences are fine. But several together become monotonous. Listen to what is happening. The writing is getting boring. The sound of it drones. It's like a stuck record. The ear demands some variety. Now listen. I vary the sentence length, and I create music. Music. The writing sings. It has a pleasant rhythm, a lilt, a harmony. I use short sentences. And I use sentences of medium length. And sometimes, when I am certain the reader is rested, I will engage him with a sentence of considerable length, a sentence that burns with energy and builds with all the impetus of a crescendo, the roll of the drums, the crash of the cymbals–sounds that say listen to this, it is important."*

Gary Provost, 100 Ways to Improve Your Writing.
See https://www.garyprovost.com/.

[41] In other words, don't start your paragraph with "Some people think X" only to wind around to say why they are wrong and why you are right. Just start by saying what the correct belief or rule is.

Bullet points where appropriate

- Bullet points lay out points in short active voice sentences or sentence fragments
- Bullet points save the reader from wading through fluff
- Bullet points separate each point for easy reading or as a checklist
  - Bullet points can have subpoints, as a way to organize within a broader point
- Bullet points can get tiring after a bit
- No one wants to read an entire book of bullet points
- So use them when appropriate, but not excessively.

15.7 Sections and their order

Your outline denotes and orders sections but that is not written in stone. Revise as needed for improved organization, order, and clarity.

Use logic and common sense for the order of sections throughout. Remember that a busy or lazy reader might not get to the end, so put the most important points first.

Sections should have a helpful and descriptive header.

The lead paragraph of the section should be direct and state the main point.

Consider what should be a main section, a sub section, and so on.

15.8 Document organization and the relationship between documents

As you outlined and planned this document, you assessed relationship. As the document evolves, revisit and revise as needed.

Avoid duplication of language across documents and properly cross-reference documents as appropriate, so organization members know what to refer to.

As you assess each document find a balance for:

- Efficiency and clarity
- Size: each document not too large or too small
- Quantity: Right number of total documents.

15.9 Edit, revise, and proofread

There are different levels of editing and proofreading, with varied focus and detail.

I like the sculpture analogy because you can imagine a sculptor carving a statue out of wood. They might start with a chainsaw, move to a large chisel, then small chisel, rough sandpaper and eventually fine sandpaper. For efficiency, there is no point using fine sandpaper in a spot if you are going to later take a chisel to that same spot.

Similarly, don't obsess over fine detail too early as you might end up deleting that sentence, paragraph, or section anyway. On the other hand, you don't want undiscovered errors lurking in the document that slip through future review. And you don't want a supervisor reviewing a draft thinking you were sloppy or lack writing skills.

Think about these things as you edit and revise:

- Message and clarity
- Readability
- Spelling
- Grammar
- Different readers, different backgrounds, different levels of familiarity
- My policy checklist
- My writing submission checklist.

As you edit and revise, consider what needs to be tracked and documented, so others know what changes were made, and so they realize you are being transparent about changes (and not trying to sneak anything in).

15.10 Put it aside, let it rest

We all reach a point where the task needs a break. Give your brain a rest, put it aside, and let your brain work on it subconsciously. When you come back to it, you will have fresh eyes and see things you didn't see before.

The period of rest should be appropriate for the project and deadline:

- Hour (have a meal or go for a walk and clear your head)
- Day
- Week
- Month

- Year (annual review).

15.11 Word count and document count[42]

As discussed earlier, consider the size of the document and number of documents.

Managing too many documents can be cumbersome. Whatever the number of documents, good organization is a key to success.

Within each document, consider:

- Number of pages
- Number of words
- Documents that are too large or cover too many subjects can be unwieldy to read and maintain
- What do we really expect the audience to read?
    - Try avoid TL;DR (Too long, didn't read).

Every person is different, as is every subject matter, but consider these rough guidelines:

- Average reading speed
    - About 200-250 words per minute
    - 100-200 for learning
    - 200-400 for comprehension
- Average speaking (presenting) speed
    - About 125-150 words per minute
- Printed page word count
    - An 8 ½ x 11 page with 1 inch margins and 12 point Times New Roman double-spaced is about 250 words per page.
    - This book can fit a maximum of about 300 words per page, but is often less depending on graphics and density of paragraphs. I am trying for a breezy read so I keep the paragraphs shorter.

15.12 Technical writing

Some governance documents are for "laypeople", and they are technically not technical writing.

---

[42] This is the arithmetic portion.

Other types of governance documents are directed at people with specialized knowledge, such as cybersecurity or IT professionals. This includes documents for cybersecurity or IT policy, standards and procedures. Similar writing principles apply, but a certain foundation of knowledge is presumed.

15.13 Writing can be "layered"

You can have "layers" to your document, with simple summaries and information up front, and more complex or more technical information behind.

In practical terms, the beginning of a document or section can have the plain-language simple takeaways, and more complex information layered in as you delve deeper.

This method will help you focus on the main points and put them up front. Assess and convey your main point early to ensure it is retained.

15.14 Keep improving yourself

We can write quality policies, procedures, and governance documents. We can do this efficiently, so that they can be read and understood efficiently.

Words are both our tools and our final product, so we can have pride in them and build our skills.

15.15 Can't AI just write for me?

Writing is hard, can't we have artificial intelligence (AI) write it for us?

My answer is no.

Remember that writing is both a process and a destination. It is not just a "deliverable", it is a process of thinking and evaluating and choosing. It is also a process of learning, of building our own skills to write, think, justify, and choose words and meaning.

Don't abdicate all of that to a tool. Take the opportunity to build yourself, and build confidence in yourself.

15.16 References and additional reading

- Policy Checklist, Chapter 26.
- Writing, https://johnbandler.com/writing/
- How to Write a Paper, https://johnbandler.com/how-to-write-paper/
- Artificial intelligence, writing and thinking, https://johnbandler.com/artificial-intelligence-writing-thinking/
- Paper submission checklist (for students, but helpful concepts for any writing), https://johnbandler.com/paper-submission-checklist/

16

Managing the documents and their evolution

In this chapter:

- Version control
- Tracking changes
- Resolving differences of opinion

16.1 Version control

You and your organization may have established protocols for managing documents through the revision process, or even have document management software systems in place. As with everything in this book, adapt my guidance to your organization's established processes.

First remember that there are two different conditions that we are tracking:

- Version control of approved and finalized versions
- Version control of unapproved drafts and the various suggestions, edits, comments as the document evolves prior to the approval.

Each condition is important for different reasons and different people.

Version control of approved versions

For approved and finalized versions, the entire organization needs to know which the current approved version is because that's what needs to be followed. It would be embarrassing if an obsolete version or unapproved version was relied upon or provided to regulators.

Someone in the organization needs to maintain the library of past approved versions, including those that are now obsolete and superseded.

In the event of a regulatory event or lawsuit, it might be relevant to know what the policy was X years ago.[43]

As always, good organization, accurate information, thoughtful, consistent filenames, and annotations within the document can help.

We will discuss file naming more as we discuss the approval and finalization of the governance document. For now, consider the merits of these filenames:

01 ORG Cybersecurity Policy 2024-08-12 Approved.docx

Just by looking at the filename, you can tell these important facts:

- Policy topic is cybersecurity
- Approved (not a draft)
- Approved on 8/12/2024

Version control of unapproved drafts

Drafts of unapproved governance documents need to be managed and tracked to avoid inefficiencies, lost work, and lost changes.

Good version control starts with thoughtful, consistent file naming.

For example:

01 ORG Cybersecurity Policy v6 2024-08-01 DRAFT.docx

With appropriate additional information in the document and established practices, this filename indicates:

- This is a draft (not approved)
- The revision date of this draft is 8/1/2024
- This is a draft of Version 6, presumably updating Version 5

Use the draft's revision date to indicate the version, rather than attempting to give version numbers to each successive draft.[44]

---

[43] As we cover later, a governance document could have a revision history within it, which makes the history available to all with revision dates and version numbers of past approved versions.

This past history is important since lawsuits can take years to be filed and progress, and may allege conduct that goes back many years. Lawyers are creative in finding reasons why documents or actions many years in the past are relevant towards whatever their claim is. An allegation of hostile work-environment might claim the organization fostered it for decades.

Within the document, clearly annotate that it is a draft (not an approved version). This should appear prominently on the first page, and can appear in multiple places, including cover page, header or footer, or even as a watermark (though I am not a fan of watermarks).

Within the document, annotate the draft version, meaning the date it was revised. For example:

> DRAFT revised 8/1/2024

Also within the document you can consider having a temporary section to note all of the prior drafts and who they were distributed to.

16.2 Collaboration

There are a number of ways multiple individuals can collaborate on a document. Depending on people and process, it can be efficient and synergistic or incredibly frustrating and time-consuming.

I think of three main ways to work on these documents:

- A single "master" version with a primary author/document manager who circulates drafts, receives and incorporates feedback (my preference)
- One "community version" that all work on, within some guidelines
- Free for all and dueling drafts (not recommended).

When many people are working on a document together it helps to have some delegation of duties and a leader of that process.[45]

If multiple people are making edits in a single document, that can be hard to resolve. Dueling edits can be a challenge. So a single document leader (manager) helps. That can be the project manager or their designee.

As a draft is circulated, others may provide:

- General suggestions or feedback
- Proposed changes

---

[44] Use the revision date to keep track of the draft version. I suggest that you do not give unapproved drafts changing version numbers because that would be too confusing in connection with the version numbers of approved documents. In other words, do not label them as draft v1, draft v2, etc.
[45] No offense to football fans, but I decided not to call this leader the "quarterback". After all, does the quarterback call the plays or does the coach?

- Comments within a document
- Tracked changes, edits within a document.

Some of that feedback may be helpful, some may need evaluation and discussion, and at times there is conflicting feedback or downright unhelpful or poor feedback.

When "tracked changes" are made by someone on the project team (or someone otherwise informed or consulted) they should be considered "tracked suggestions", and then the project team needs to decide whether those changes are incorporated, adapted, or rejected.

I recommend the review cycle as we previewed earlier in Chapter 13. The document manager sends out the draft, properly annotated, and solicits feedback and thus:

- Project team (or any others consulted) provide feedback as instructed or however they please (email, phone, tracked changes, comments, etc.)
- Document manager receives all feedback and consolidates and addresses
- Document manager maintains the "master" version and ultimately will send out a revised draft.

We'll talk about resolving differences of opinion later, and for now assume the suggestions and edits are all reasonable and without dissent, or that a reasonable consensus can be achieved and someone with significant authority can make the final decision.

Assuming the project team desires transparency in changes, the document manager should turn on "track changes" for their master version, and input the changes provided by other team members. They can also comment as needed to explain or attribute suggestions to a particular person.[46]

---

[46] Since the person managing the document is inputting the suggestions into their master document version, the tracked changes feature will show as the manager's change. Comments can make clear whose suggested change it is. The alternative is when everyone edits and comments in a shared document, but that can get very cluttered and confusing. After many books and receiving hundreds of documents with tracked changes and comments, I am accustomed to having my "master" version on the right side of the screen, the suggestions version on the left side, and scrolling through to address comments.

When an issue is discussed and resolved, it can be helpful to leave a comment to briefly annotate. As the document is circulated further, new readers might have similar questions, and this can save time, reducing the need for questions to be re-asked and re-answered.

Remember that project team "tracked changes" are just suggestions until there is an appropriate decision or consensus about what changes should be implemented (accepted).

If changes are going to be made, the "tracked change" feature lets all project team members know what changes were made by the document manager.

Eventually, these tracked changes can become clutter that needs to be cleared by "accepting" those changes. Otherwise, it can become confusing to understand which is a prior change that has already been reviewed and circulated, and which is a new change for review.

Keep in mind that if this document is a revision of a prior version, then the approving authority will need to know the net changes are since the last approved version, but will probably not care about the various interim unapproved drafts and the changes within them.

The "compare" feature can be used to compare the last approved version to the "near final draft" version which is submitted for approval.

16.3 The document manager (a human)

It makes sense for the project manager to manage the documents. They are already managing the project, the document is the deliverable of the project, so there is efficiency by having these be the same person.

Perhaps the project manager is juggling many responsibilities, in which case the project manager could delegate this duty to a subordinate or trusted colleague.

I knew that any time a document came back to me from another person, there might be untracked changes, autoformat or autocorrect settings applied, or any number of other issues. By maintaining my master version and inputting changes myself it eliminated confusion and saved time in the long run.

While it may seem like taking on extra work for the project manager to also be the document manager, it can save time and add efficiency. As always, consider the human factor—the way this is conducted matters.[47]

Even if the organization uses a "document manager" software or platform, there should be a human overseeing the flow of changes and evolution of this document.

16.4 A protocol for document management[48]

These are my preferences for managing documents, which I have found save time and reduce confusion for both me and clients.

- I try to solicit thoughts and gain consensus on smaller issues or details in advance of a more complete draft.
  - o This approach reduces the number of uncertainties when the first draft is sent, and reduces the number of subsequent tracked changes.
- I control the "master version" of the document
- I send out periodic updates or drafts for review, feedback, work
- My updates are sent by email with
  - o Clear subject
  - o Brief summary for a busy reader
  - o More details if the reader has time
  - o List the filename in the body
- Each draft is clearly marked as a draft and has important version information
  - o In the filename (words "draft" and the revision date in format YYYY-MM-DD)
  - o Within the document, readily viewable when previewed, opened, or printed to paper

---

[47] As alluded to earlier, each organization may have undercurrents and interpersonal or interdepartmental politics and turf wars. On the one hand some individuals might *not* want additional work and responsibilities to manage feedback and the document. On the other hand, they might not like it if they think someone else is trying to grab this work. The same person might react in opposite fashions depending on how the matter is proposed.

[48] Adjust for your situation and organization. This works well for me, but remember that I am always outside the organization, an external attorney or consultant hired to help them with their policy work. If you are inside the organization you need to consider your processes and who you report to.

- I collect input from anyone and everyone willing to provide, in whatever format is convenient for them
- I input any changes or comments myself into the "master version"
- I create frequent revisions of the "master version" by doing a "save as" and changing the date contained within the filename.

16.5 Filename preferences

As previously covered , my preferred filename is something like:

01 ORG Cybersecurity Policy v6 rev 2024-08-22 DRAFT.docx

Here's the key to the format:

- 01 = optional sorting field. Whatever works in your organization. Here, it is 01 for the highest cybersecurity document
- ORG = optional organization name or abbreviation (if that's the way you do it)
- Cybersecurity Policy — Identifies this document
- vX= Identify the version this draft will be, once approved
- Rev = indicates the date that follows is a revision date (optional)
- 2024-MM-DD — The date of this version.
  - Note that with YYYY-MM-DD, your versions will sort chronologically as long as all the preceding characters stay the same.[49]
    If you have multiple versions on the same date you can add a time at the end.
- DRAFT — Tells everyone that this is a DRAFT!

Spending just a little time and thought on the filename can save a lot of confusion, especially because you do not know how far any document will be circulated, how each person will store it, and whether they will dig it up and provide it to someone in the future.[50]

---

[49] Try this YYYY-MM-DD filename convention out for a while and you will get used to it and see the benefits. I know it may seem different, but the advantages of chronological sorting become clear soon enough. Let's face it, other formats, like MM-DD-YYYY or DD-MM-YYYY or even Month Year don't provide those sorting benefits.
[50] Imagine an employee providing a draft, unapproved document to a regulator, thinking it is in force. It has happened for sure.

16.6 Document versioning annotations

Include prominent annotations within the document so when it is previewed, opened or printed to PDF or paper, it is clearly marked as a draft version with the revision date.

Even if the reader overlooks the filename (or you forget to update the filename) the document clearly indicates the draft status in these places:

- Cover page (if it exists)
- Anywhere version information might be or should be
  - Cover page
  - Right under the policy title, if there is no cover page
- Header/footer (if it contains version info)
- Revision history (if contained within document)
- Revision history of this draft (if applicable)
- Watermark? (I am not a fan of watermarks, but other people seem to like them).

Cover page

Here is a sample cover page of a draft and unapproved policy.[51]

Notice the prominent placing of the word "DRAFT" and "NOT APPROVED YET", so that the status of this document is clear. Further, there are placeholders so that when this document is eventually approved and then finalized, the person knows they will need to include the approval date.

Also notice the revision date on the cover. As multiple revisions may be flying around, some printed to paper, some visible in a "preview pane" prior to opening the document, it is easy to see the draft version based on the revision date.

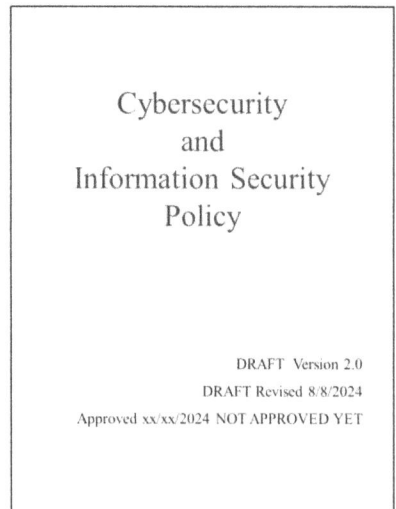

> Cybersecurity
> and
> Information Security
> Policy
>
> DRAFT Version 2.0
> DRAFT Revised 8/8/2024
> Approved xx/xx/2024 NOT APPROVED YET

---

[51] The fonts are not to scale since I enlarged them for the purpose of the diagram.

Revision history

Here is a sample annotation within the document revision history section of approved versions as the organization works on the next update.

Revision History					
Version	Policy Implemented By	Revision Date	Approved By	Approval Date	Comment
1.0	Information Security Coordinator	04/01/2023	CEO	04/01/2023	New cybersecurity policy.
2.0	Information Security Coordinator	DRAFT REVISED 08/08/2024	CEO	NOT APPROVED YET	Annual update and improvements to policy.

From a glance you can tell what the last approved version is, that this is an unapproved draft, the revision date, who is in charge of the policy and who is the approver.

You can also see the placeholders that will need to be adjusted to finalize the document once it is approved.

Revision history of draft unapproved versions

Here is a sample annotation that is a temporary table showing the revision history of the draft, unapproved versions.

REVISION HISTORY OF THIS DRAFT ** REMOVE BEFORE FINALIZING **			
Draft of Version	Draft date	Circulated to	Comment
2.0	4/1/2024	Larry, Moe, Curly	First draft of v 2.0 circulated to team to check basics, fill in some blanks, answer initial questions.
2.0	5/4/2024	Larry, Moe, Curly	Second draft circulated, incorporated suggested edits (see comments throughout)
2.0			
2.0			
2.0			

This lets project team members know what drafts were circulated, when, and to whom. Obviously, this will be removed from the final, approved version, and can be removed even before that as the document gets closer to approval.

16.7 Receiving and reviewing feedback

The document manager may receive feedback from many different individuals, it may be provided in different ways, and sometimes they agree and sometimes they conflict.

Have your "master version" ready and review the feedback one at a time.

- Master document to one side of screen (e.g. right side, keep it consistent)
- Feedback/comment document to other (e.g., left side)
- Review the feedback, and change or annotate that master version as appropriate
- Comment as needed
- Respond to individual as needed, or make a note to respond to the entire project team.

16.8 Distributing drafts for the review cycle

Periodically circulate drafts to necessary individuals. Email is usually convenient for this, and consider these points:

- Subject
- Greeting
- Information about this draft
- Paste the filename into the body of the email (which also has the version info in it)
- Say how to provide feedback (e.g., however convenient)
- Deadline (soft or firm, up front or at the end)
- Pleasant signoff.

16.9 Communicating with the project team

Remember you are communicating with people (see Chapter 12) and here's some main principles for working well with your project team:

- Communicate
- Better to overcommunicate than under communicate
  - Solicit input
  - Advise of developments
- Try to layer your communications
  - Simple important information up front for a quick read
  - Details later
- Check yourself for content and tone
  - Consider the human element.

Generally, it is better to overcommunicate than under communicate, so long as you do not do it in an annoying or harassing way.

When you provide adequate or slightly excessive communications, some might not want to be bothered, say "go ahead" and "do whatever". In the back of their mind, they know you have been providing a lot of information and they have the option of not reading your communications. These are all positive points.

If you under communicate, they might feel you are not sharing enough, not doing your duty to communicate, or worse might get suspicious that you are hiding something. They start wanting to know more details and may view things differently or adversely. Remember that they don't have the option of reading a communication you never sent.

Use appropriate communication methods for the circumstances, which may include:

- Email
- Phone
- Text
- Video conference
- In-person.

Be mindful of organization norms and rules for communication and communication preservation. Consider personal preferences, and if one method is not working effectively or does not get any response, try another.

Try and target communications appropriate to the issue or sub-issue, including:

- Full project group
- Subproject or task group
- One-to-one.

Work to select appropriate level of detail within each communication:

- Short
- Medium
- Long
- Layered (short, then more)
    - Provide short summary up front (TLDR) with critical information
    - Then provide more details below, for anyone who wants to read it, or as a note to file.

Communication helps meet deadlines or avoid excessive delays. Check-in throughout the process and before a deadline, and follow-up after a deadline has passed.

Try and avoid these unless necessary:

> ✗ *This is late!*
>
> ✗ *When are you getting this in?*

These might be more appropriate:

> ✓ *I wanted to see how this was going and when you thought you could get it in?*
>
> ✓ *I wanted to check in on how things were going, if you had any questions, needed anything, and make sure the future task deadline of 8/8/2024 was on your calendar and radar.*

Consider the way you communicate and how it might be received, and think about this quote:

> *People will forget what you said.*
>
> *People will forget what you did.*
>
> *But people will never forget how you made them feel.*
>
> *— Maya Angelou*

And then consider this variation for emails you send and documents you create:

> *People will forget what you wrote but the information system won't.*
>
> *— John Bandler*

As you communicate, think about these things:

- Consider their perspective and feelings (empathy and respect)
- Consider their position, title and power (affects you and your career!)
- Consider it may be a lasting record (for good or for bad).

Some people are notoriously afraid of putting things in writing, for fear that it might come back to "bite them" someday. Just remember that email is an important form of communication, so clear, accurate emails can vastly improve your document project and organization.

Email communications

Remember that emails should have these parts:

- Appropriate tone (when in doubt, wait before sending)
- Clear
- Proofread for clarity, spelling, punctuation, tone
- Subject: Relevant to the message
- Initial greeting: Pleasant and identify who you are sending it to
- Longish email? Layer the message for busy readers
  - Brief initial summary up front of important bits
  - Details later
- Note any attachments (including filename)
- Sign-off pleasantly.

16.10 Resolving differences of opinion

Choices will need to be made and differences of opinion will occur. Sometimes they are easy to resolve, sometimes it can seem like an impossible logjam. Good decision making principles apply here regarding which option will work best (or choosing another course).

Some basic steps to resolve these differences include:

- Isolate the issues
  - Identify where people agree
  - Identify where they disagree and the underlying reasoning
  - Sometimes this requires some analysis
- Identify the options
- Identify the pros and cons of each option.

Who decides?

Depending on who decides and their management style, resolving differences of opinion can be simple.

> *We are doing it this way.*

Or simple with explanation:

> *We are doing it this way because EXPLAIN.*
> *Thank you for your feedback and thoughts which helps*
> *with the process.*

Or, the project team may need to reach a consensus together so they can all agree when they present it to the ultimate approving authority in the organization.

Nothing is truly "decided" until the document approver(s) approve that document. Changes could be inserted at any point.

If this is an important issue, it could be something for the document approver to consider in advance of submitting the document for approval.

Isolate the issues

Where there is disagreement, the issues need to be isolated and separated. Sometimes people disagree vehemently but do not state specifically what they disagree with, nor suggest ways to correct it to make it more acceptable.

The key is to isolate issues to ease decision-making and reduce conflict. First, try to understand the areas of disagreement, and these phrases can help:

> *What exactly isn't right? (and why)*
>
> *What changes would make it better?*

With this, you may find areas of agreement. You can zoom in (or out) to the appropriate level of detail to identify issues. Is it with:

- The document in general
- A section
- A paragraph
- A sentence
- A phrase in a sentence
- A word.

As discussed throughout the book, modularity helps. If sections, paragraphs, and sentences are structured well, it is easier to focus on areas of agreement and disagreement, and how to fix it.

If a single sentence tries to make three different points, and there is disagreement about that sentence, break it into three simple sentences and isolate where the issues lie.

Ideally you work to resolve more general (larger) issues first. If you can't first agree on whether you are driving to Los Angeles or Chicago, there is no point discussing which car or route to take. Address finer levels of detail as more general areas are resolved.

As with our section on decision making, consider:

- Big issues first
- Address "threshold" issues first
  - Whatever point you are at now, there are probably issues that need to be resolved first, before getting to other issues.
- Make decisions and develop consensus
- Avoid backtracking by thoroughly considering options the first time and involving the right people
- Address finer levels of detail.

Develop options

When you have isolated an issue, develop options. It can be helpful when brainstorming to consider even unreasonable extreme options, since this can help you focus on the more reasonable options. It also helps you identify the reasonable edges and unreasonable extremes on both sides.

Realize and acknowledge that reasonable people can disagree, and there may be a range of reasonable, justifiable options.

But also realize that some people are *not* reasonable, and some people might not state their true reasoning or motives. Avoid situations where people present false choices or skew the pros and cons to try induce the outcome they want.

Examine pros and cons

Examine pros, cons and the risks of each option. You can ask each proponent to explain their reasoning and underlying issues, including pros and cons and their perceived risks.

As with politics, proponents who only see the merits of their own suggestion (and no downsides) and only see the detriments of other options (with no upsides) may be either less than objective or less than candid, or both.

Prioritize the reasoning, benefits and risks, and remember that not every pro and con is of equal priority or weight.

Priority should be granted to aligning documents with external rules. Whatever the dispute about language, if the external rule requires something then the internal rule must comply with it and cannot conflict with it.

Secondary priority should also be given to mission and directing proper practice. This means being realistic, clear, and practical.

Remember these principles:

- Internal rules should align with external rules
- If external rules require certain things to be in the internal rules, the internal rules should have them
- Internal rules should align with mission
- Internal rules should direct the proper practice
- Improper practice does *not* dictate the internal rules.

Don't fall into these traps:

> ✘ *We can't make that a policy requirement because we aren't currently doing that.*

> ✘ *Such a policy would mean we are immediately out of compliance with our own policy, so we can't do that.*

This is tail-wags-the-dog logic which should not stand. An organization's management sets policy based on what action should be, then action needs to follow that policy. Not vice-versa.

Nor this:

> ✘ *This document is a rule so it must be written with all 'musts' and rigid requirements.*

Remember that most rules require some exercise of judgment and common sense, as employees interpret and act, and as the organization enforces its rules. The writing needs to be readable.

Nor these:

> ✘ *This external rule requires a voluminous policy covering every single possible circumstance.*

> ✘ *Employees are the worst and will misunderstand or deliberately misunderstand everything unless we spell it out fifteen different ways.*

> ✘ *We need a voluminous policy covering every single possible circumstance.*

> ✘ *We need an internal rule for each external rule.*

Yes, external rules, mission and protection will require internal rules and documentation. Yes, people can misunderstand.

That said, the degree of documentation needs to be thoughtfully crafted, so think about efficiency and goals, and do not just create documents and words for the sake of completeness.

Since every document is not just for compliance (but for action and mission), we generally don't name documents after the law. After all, we want to address that topic area properly, and there might be multiple laws we need to comply with in any single topic area.

If your state has a new privacy law, you certainly want to comply with it, and you probably need to create some governance documentation, but the focus is privacy and protecting consumer privacy, not whatever the name of the new privacy law is.

16.11 References

- Chapter 26, Policy Checklist
- Version control, https://johnbandler.com/version-control

17

Gaining approval and finalizing the document

In this chapter:

- Gain consensus in advance for efficiency and feedback
- Submitting for approval
- Last minute changes
- Finalizing

17.1 Gain consensus long in advance of the approval request

Whenever possible, gain consensus and "socialize" the policy document well in advance of any requests for approval.

Ideally, the approver is involved in the project process to some degree throughout the project process, or trusted advisors of the approver are involved in the project throughout. By the time the document gets to the approval process there should be agreement on the major issues and hopefully minor issues too.

If the approver is not part of the project process and is a management grade above the project team, and if culture is not optimal, inefficiencies can result. The project team should do their best as the project progresses, but some things may be out of their control.[52]

---

[52] Imagine a busy approver who does not want to be involved in the project and says, "Show me what you have when you are done" and "Don't bother me with this until you are done." The project team spends hours and weeks and months and wrestles with issues big and small, and eventually sends the near-final draft for approval, and one of two things might happen.

If the approver approves "as-is" or with minor changes upon sufficient consultation, then everything went efficiently. But if the approver gets out the red pen and makes large changes on matters the team previously discussed or deliberated about, then that means much backtracking will occur with considerable inefficiency. So better to have the approver on board early.

17.2 Submitting for approval

When a governance document is submitted for approval, this is the final and ultimate review cycle.

The approving authority might be an individual, group of individuals, or a formal committee.

Hopefully, the approvers have been following along with the process, have trust in the project manager and people submitting the document(s) for approval, have been incrementally approving major decision points and will not impose extreme changes at the last minute.

Remember that an efficient policy project process is one where the documents move steadily towards completion, without major backtracks or reversals. If extreme changes are imposed at the last minute that can mean inefficiency and might be a sign that certain conditions were not properly considered during the process.

The submission can include one or more of these things:

- Proposed document in near-final clean draft version (revision date clear and its status as an unapproved draft clear)
    - It is not a "final" nor "final version" nor "final draft"
    - It is an "unapproved" draft, and perhaps "near final draft"
    - Filename could be something like: 01 ORGNAME Cybersecurity Policy vX 2024-MM-DD DRAFT for approval.docx
- If an update to an existing document: Summary of any changes (appropriate level of detail)
- If a new document: Summary of what the document is and why it is needed (appropriate level of detail)
- Verbal presentation
- Slide deck (PowerPoint) presentation
- Redlined version (showing word-by-word changes between prior approved version and this proposed version).[53]

During approval discussion some foundational questions may arise, so it can be helpful to restate or recap some of the broader goals such as:

---

[53] The approving authority will likely not care about changes during the drafting process, so remove or reduce that type of clutter. Focus on changes between the last approved version and this update.

- Mission and efficiency
- Comply with external rules
- Protect the organization.

Realize that communication with the approving authority may be filtered and things may get lost in the translation, especially if you are not in direct communication with the approving authority.

Where disagreements arise among the approving authority, try to:

- Identify what people agree on
- Identify the precise areas of disagreement
- Why they disagree
- Proposed fix, and why that is better
- Identify pros, cons, and risks.

Ultimately the approving authority will decide along one of three basic lines:

- Not approved. Needs more work and resubmission.
- Approved as-is
- Approved subject to a few minor changes.

Let's talk through each scenario briefly.

Not approved yet — Additional changes needed

If the document is not approved and additional changes are needed, then the project manager should obtain appropriate guidance for the changes, document them (e.g. with an email or memo) circulate them and commence another review cycle.

When the document is presented again for approval, the changes will need to be clear (e.g. redlined) and with a summary of how the changes satisfy the requirements from the approving authority.

Approved as-is!

If the document is approved as-is, note the date and approving authority, and you can commence finalizing it (see next).

Approved subject to a few minor changes

If the document is approved subject to some additional changes, consider the importance and impact of the changes when deciding to what degree those changes need to be documented.

For example, are the desired changes specified via verbal conversation, meeting minutes, email, memo, or redlined document?

If needed, an email can be circulated to confirm the changes desired, or as a further step another "near-final draft" can be circulated showing the new changes.

The situation you want to avoid is a misunderstanding, or approver(s) later believing or claiming:

That's not the policy I approved.

I didn't approve that change.

That change was made after I approved the document.

A simple email can avoid future misunderstanding and is available to review even after time passes and recollections fade.

17.3 Documenting a verbal approval

If approval is given verbally, it can be confirmed in writing, such as with an email.

Dear O Wondrous approver[s],

Nice to see you today. This email confirms that you [the XYZ committee] approved the Super Duper Policy v. 2 today (8/8/2024). I will note this approval date in the document when I finalize it shortly and will distribute that finalized document.

All best,

Super Duper Policy Project Manager

Adjust as needed to suit your organization and culture.

17.4 Starting to finalize—Almost there

With approval gained, you take your master version and do another save as" and update the filename date to indicate it is another near-final draft. Then incorporate any last-minute changes (hopefully very minor) and clean up the document by resolving any outstanding tracked changes and comments.

Ideally, the revision process has been such that any pending tracked changes should be "accepted". If there is doubt regarding what should be accepted or rejected, that may require additional communication to ensure the finalized policy reflects what was approved.

While resolving comments, you may need to clean the master document and copy out certain issues which were tabled for another time, so that it can be raised during the next update (and not forgotten about).

Within the document, include approval information and date approved, and remove any "draft" annotations.

With a cleaner document, there should not be any annotations, comments, or tracked changes remaining.

Now it is time to perform a final proofreading, check pagination, spacing, and formatting. Don't get carried away with edits and don't change anything substantive, since the document is already approved.

17.5 Finalizing—Mark it "approved"

Now it is time to make it final—mark it as the "approved" document.

Do a "Save as" again, now with a filename indicating it is the approved version, e.g.:

01 ORG Cybersecurity Policy vX 2024-MM-DD Approved.docx

Where the date is the approval date.

Then do another "Save as" to PDF format.

Make them both "read-only".

Using the word "Approved" is a single clean word that clearly distinguishes this from all the prior drafts, and avoids the confusion that comes with using the word "final".[54]

Take another look through your PDF, to make sure it looks good, the page breaks and formatting are OK, and that you didn't miss anything in a prior proofreading.

If you have a project team, you can circulate the document to them first, in case there are any errors you missed.

---

[54] Remember that many people incorrectly use the word "final" in circumstances where it is not really the final. Using "approved" saves that confusion. But if you have to use the word "final", this would be the one time to use it, and consider:
01 ORG Cybersecurity Policy vX 2024-MM-DD Final Approved.docx
And I recommend avoiding this:
✗ 01 ORG Cybersecurity Policy vX 2024-MM-DD Final.docx

The PDF would be the "official" version of the approved policy, and appropriate people should also have access to the word processing version (e.g., DOCX) for the next update. If you are an outside consultant or lawyer, be sure to give them the document version so they are not hostage to you for the next update.

Now that it's final, the next step is to publish, distribute, train, and implement.

17.6 References

- Approval and finalizing of organization documents, https://johnbandler.com/approval-finalizing-documents/
- Chapter 26 Policy Checklist

18

Publication, training, implementation

In this chapter:

- Publication
- Training and acknowledgment
- Implementation

We have an approved, finalized document but we are not done!

It can't just sit somewhere in secret gathering dust.

It is time for the next steps.

18.1 Publish and distribute

Now it's time to distribute the finalized document to everywhere it needs to go. (Before this, you had your project team or trusted colleagues check your work to find any last mistakes).

Organizations may have their own processes for storing governance documents and for notifying employees of changes.

If there is a central repository, the newly approved document needs to be placed there. If it updates and replaces a prior document, that obsolete document should be removed, as appropriate.[55]

---

[55] From the employee perspective, they need to be able to quickly find *current* governance documents without confusion about which version is current or obsolete. This means employees should not have to wade through obsolete documents. Get them out of there to avoid misunderstandings.

Still, someone in the organization needs to track and maintain past, approved versions. There needs to be a repository of all approved governance documents, including obsolete policies and procedures. It should be clear which documents are in force and which have been superseded (made obsolete). In the event of a

Employees who fall under the new or updated governance document should be notified about the changes. This can be done through one or more of the following steps:

- Email about the new policy/updated document
- Include a copy of the document
- Include a link or mention of where the document is stored
- A brief summary of the new document or new changes
- A brief persuasion on the importance of the document
- A training (see next section)
- An acknowledgement (see next section).

These are some of the things we want to avoid:

- Employees or managers not knowing the document exists
- Employees or managers not knowing the new rules exist
- Employees or managers not following the new rules.

From a compliance perspective, organizations have a certain duty to train and supervise employees. Putting a compliance-oriented policy in place without providing sufficient notice or training is not a viable approach. If an organization never notifies employees about a policy, others might claim it is a shadow policy or even a sham policy.

From a business goals perspective, organizations want employees to do what they are supposed to.

18.2 Training and (or) acknowledgement

Notifying employees of a new or updated governance document is an initial step and may be sufficient in some instances.

In some organizations or situations an acknowledgement may be required, or a training, or both. As always, we can look to the concept of reasonableness under the circumstances, and balance mission, efficiency, compliance, and a duty to train and supervise employees.

Organizations need to ensure employees have paid sufficient attention to the policy. This can be accomplished through training and/or acknowledgement. This aids in compliance and rebuts the following potential accusations:

---

lawsuit or regulatory issue, the organization needs to know what documents were in place on what dates.

Your organization didn't train your employees.

Your organization didn't take that policy seriously, or expect employees to follow it.

It also reduces or rebuts the following employee statements:

I didn't know about that policy.

No one told me about that policy.

I never saw the email about that policy.

I never checked the repository about that policy.

You didn't give me time to read it.

You didn't train me on it.

Some ways to accomplish this training and acknowledgment step include:

- Email the new documents
- Require an email response acknowledging receipt and reading of the new documents
- Upload to an organization training/learning platform to ensure that employees review and acknowledge
- Hold a training
- Obtain acknowledgement after the training
- Obtain acknowledgment and have a mini-quiz after the training.

The most effective training is informative and not painful. But let's be realistic, it is a work related training (not entertainment).

The trainers should be persuasive about the new governance document's importance for both mission and compliance. They should never downplay it, demean it, nor diminish the message. This is not bureaucratic work, checking boxes or shelfware, but an important document that supports the organization.

The organization is about people and what they do, and that's why the organization is investing time and resources to train and inform them about what the laws and rules are.

18.3 Other implementation

Other implementation measures may be required. For example, this newly approved document might require changes to other, lower documents so they comply with it.

If the organization is using governance, risk, and compliance (GRC) software tools, they might need reconfiguration so that they properly comply with the new documents or changes.

If the new documents require significant changes in practices there might need to be a work plan to get all those changes made. And if the new documents impose changes that need to be reflected in other documents, those documents should be updated.

Implementation checklist

To implement a new document consider these items:

- Final versions properly named and properly stored
    - o PDF version is the "official" version and available for the organization
    - o Word processor version (e.g. docx) available for those who might need it in the future for updates
    - o Both are made "read only"
- Obsolete (superseded) versions removed from the main employee library (or clearly marked as obsolete) and archived for compliance purposes
- Employees properly notified
- Employees acknowledge new document
- Employees properly trained
- Employees acknowledge training or otherwise it is tracked
- New document properly incorporated for any:
    - o Audit
    - o Cross-walking, mapping, integrating
    - o Laws, frameworks
    - o Compliance tools
    - o Configuration tools
    - o Work plan created if needed to complete implementation and identify future steps.

18.4 We are done?

Policy work—like management—is never "done". It is a continual process as we will discuss in the next chapter.

This is a good time to think about what the next steps would be and put a reminder on the calendar noting when the annual review or update process should start.

When the policy project is complete, we need to recognize that a lot of effort was put into it by the project team, and some type of acknowledgement is beneficial. Depending on the size of the project the following actions might be appropriate:

- Private thanks to those who helped with the project
    - Phone call
    - Email
    - Letter of appreciation
    - Token of appreciation
- Public acknowledgement of efforts of those on the team
- Lunch
- After work event
- Party
- More formal after-action review of the project.

18.5 References

- Publication, training, and implementation, https://johnbandler.com/publication-training-implementation/

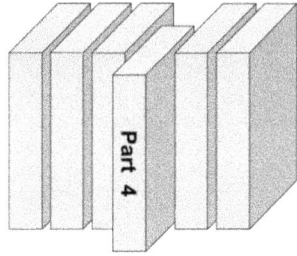

Part 4

Cybersecurity policy work

A part with three chapters specific to cybersecurity policies.

- Cybersecurity laws
- Cybersecurity external guidance
  - Including the Four Pillars of Cybersecurity

→ → → → → → → → → → → → → → → →

⏩ Skippable if your project has nothing to do with cybersecurity.

19

Cybersecurity laws and external rules

In this chapter:

- Cybersecurity basics
- Cyberlaw recap
- Negligence theory
- Contract theory (insurance too)
- Federal vs state
- Sector specific

This chapter helps you with a cybersecurity related governance document.

Skip if your document has nothing to do with cybersecurity.

➔ ➔ ➔ ➔ ➔ ➔ ➔ ➔ ➔ ➔ ➔ ➔ ➔ ➔ ➔ ➔

▶▶ Skippable if you are not working on cybersecurity.

19.1 Cybersecurity basics

Here's some cybersecurity basics to get you started.[56]

Information security is the process of protecting information, whatever form that information takes. Cybersecurity is a newer and essential

---

[56] Why do we need a section on cybersecurity basics just to learn about cybersecurity laws?

Imagine taking a class on traffic law and you didn't know the basics of a car, what the steering wheel does, what the pedals do, what a crash entails, and etc.

Imagine being a hotel owner and taking a class on premises liability law, and you want to have a safe hotel for customers, but you don't know how to close a door or lock a door, and you have never heard of video surveillance.

Similarly, to understand cybersecurity law we need to know some basics about cybersecurity.

subset of information security, focused on protecting information assets in digital form, and also protecting from cybercrime. Information security is a concept that has been around for thousands of years.

Cybersecurity starts with people and the decisions they make to manage risk. The risks include cybercrime and natural disaster. The three main cybercrimes to know about and protect against are:

- Data breach
- Ransomware
- Email based funds transfer frauds (business email compromise, CEO fraud).

There are three main objectives of cybersecurity, remember them with "CIA":

- *Confidentiality* means keeping unauthorized users from accessing the systems or data.
- *Integrity* means that only authorized users can make changes.
- *Availability* means that authorized users can access their systems and data when needed.

To achieve the three objectives, organizations (and individuals) should apply appropriate controls, also known as safeguards. You can remember these with the initialism of "PAT":

- *Physical* controls restrict physical access in one way or another.
- *Administrative* controls include rules, policies, and training.
- *Technical* controls are electronic protections, such as a firewall, antivirus, or monitoring software.

Notice here the importance of administrative controls like policies and procedures. That's our wheelhouse!

Cybersecurity has some simple basic principles which you need to apply to secure your office or home. You also need a basic understanding of technology.

There are many best practices (external guidance) available to help individuals and organizations manage their cybersecurity. We discuss that in following chapters.

19.2 Cyberlaw (recap)

Remember from our introduction to cyberlaw in Chapter 5 that it encompasses the large bodies of traditional law we may already be familiar with, including criminal, negligence, and contract law. Then we layer in some additional data specific laws including:

- Data disposal (securely disposing of consumer data)
- Data breach reporting (report data breaches to government and consumers)
- Cybersecurity (protect consumer data, and protect the organization)
- Privacy (many duties regarding consumers and their privacy).

Some of these rules come from the federal government, some from the states. Some apply only to specific sectors such as health, finance, or education, and some apply generally to almost all organizations.

Our earlier diagram showed these four components separately and now it is time to evolve the diagram one step further by showing that most privacy laws will include provisions on cybersecurity and breach notification, as depicted in the diagram.

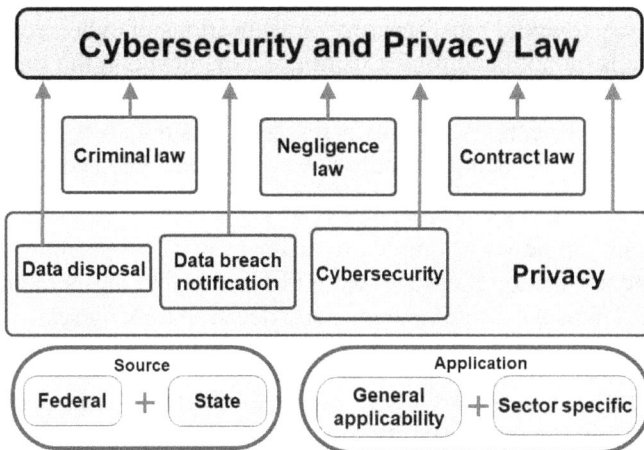

Cybersecurity and Privacy Law (2)

While a law might require cybersecurity only for consumer data, good business practices and fulfilling the mission requires organizations to have good cybersecurity for all their information systems.

Note that some sector-specific laws do require good cybersecurity throughout the organization. For example, by law, a bank needs to have effective cybersecurity to protect consumer data *and* to ensure the bank can continue operations, as a regulated part of our country's critical infrastructure.

19.3 Negligence and cybersecurity

Negligence is an important and longstanding body of law. My mantra for clients is:

> *Be reasonable and diligent.*
>
> *Don't be negligent or sloppy.*

Who can argue with that, regardless of the underlying topic? No good business wants to think of itself as being negligent or sloppy in any way.

Remember that the elements of a negligence claim are:

- A duty is owed
- Breach of that duty (failed to exercise reasonable care)
- That breach caused damages (monetary loss).

With cybersecurity, the organization wants to be able to show that its cybersecurity was sufficient, reasonable, and diligent.

The best way to avoid most scrutiny or accusations of cybersecurity negligence is by not becoming a victim of cybercrime in the first place. This means having sufficient cybersecurity to prevent incidents and protect against threats. While this is the goal, it is not always possible, and the mere fact of being a victim does not prove cybersecurity negligence.

The analysis can be very complex to discover what cybersecurity and cybercrime prevention measures were in place before an incident. Was it reasonable? Was their risk tolerance and decision making reasonable? We can never eliminate all risk, but we can responsibly manage risk.

Cybersecurity policies are there to ensure the organization is diligent and reasonable with its cybersecurity program.

19.4 Contract and cybersecurity

The elements of a valid contract are:

- Offer
- Acceptance of that offer
- Exchange of something of value ("consideration"), and

- The contract does not violate the law or principles of good society ("public policy").

Many contracts require appropriate cybersecurity and privacy, as there may be duties, promises, representations, disclaimers, waivers, and indemnification.

Organizations may have a duty to implement certain cybersecurity measures, to detect, investigate, and notify of cybercrime attacks, breaches, and more.

Terms of Use, Terms of Service, and Privacy Policies are all contracts, creating obligations for the organization and customers.

Insurance policies, including "cyber insurance" are contracts that impose duties on both parties, including for the organization to have accurately disclosed information about the company, and to promptly report cyber events to the insurer.

Where these types of legal duties exist, it may be worthwhile to clearly note that in the cybersecurity policy and incident response plan.

When the organization enters into contracts with others, it should evaluate what duties are being imposed upon the organization, and what duties should be imposed on others with respect to cybersecurity, notification, investigation, and privacy.

When organizations share data with each other, there should be a contractual obligation that addresses issues of cybersecurity, cybercrime investigation, and privacy. The organization should also consider indemnification, insurance requirements, and limitations of liability.

When organizations enter into agreements with payment processors, there will typically be contractual requirements regarding security and crime prevention.[57]

---

[57] These contractual provisions may provide for overlap between some of our policy components. For example, a credit card processing merchant agreement might contractually obligate a party to comply with a cybersecurity framework, such as the Payment Card Industry Data Security Standard (PCI-DSS). External guidance now becomes an external rule.

19.5 Assessment of applicable cybersecurity external rules

The organization needs to assess what external rules apply to it regarding cybersecurity and privacy, and this is an area with a patchwork of laws according to jurisdiction and sector.

Location

They want to consider their geographic location, including:

- States with headquarters and offices
- States with employees
- States with customers and clients.

Depending on the situation this can be simple or complex. Sometimes it requires prioritizing. The states to consider first are the states where the organization is headquartered and those with the dominant footprint or contacts. Also consider the states with the strictest laws, because complying with those puts you in good stead for all the others.

This can seem overwhelming, but we need to prioritize our time and make steady steps forward. As we consider decision making principles and options, we can see some extremes to rule out and a middle option that is more reasonable.

> ✗ *Decide it is too complicated, do nothing.*
>
> ✓ *Expend reasonable resources (time, money) to make solid progress to identify applicable laws, definitions, and terminology.*
>
> ✗ *Spend excessive resources (time, money) to analyze every word of every potential statute, cross reference, and let FUD take over as you decide on policy language and zigzag back and forth among various options.*

Sector and type of work

Organizations should consider their sector of work and various licenses their employees hold, including:

- Health and medical
- Finance
- Utilities
- Education
- Defense or government contracting
- Law and legal
- Any sector that is part of "critical infrastructure".

Each area may have specific laws and regulations that apply to it, enforced by different regulators. Keep in mind that each sector has differing risks. Generally, when a sector or profession is licensed and regulated, the regulatory body has probably recognized the importance of cybersecurity and issued rules about it.

One component of these cybersecurity laws is protecting consumer information from data breach and protecting people from being victimized by cybercrime and identity theft.

Another component is protecting critical infrastructure from cyber-attack. It is in the best interest of our country to be protected and resilient from such attacks from nation states, terrorists, or common criminals.

19.6 A few external rules to consider

FTC Act

The Federal Trade Commission (FTC) Act (among many other provisions) empowers the FTC to regulate unfair or deceptive trade practices.[58] This power has evolved to include the general principle that companies should have fair and clear privacy practices, hold data with a certain level of security and not make deceptive claims about their level of security.[59] Thus, the FTC is a primary federal enforcer of privacy and cybersecurity requirements.

Remember that there is no general specific federal law on cybersecurity, data breach reporting, or privacy, but the FTC Act pretty much fills that role for now. There are separate specific federal laws that apply to certain sectors such as finance and health.

NY State

New York's SHIELD Act (passed in 2019) strengthened existing data breach notification rules and imposed a new "reasonable cybersecurity" requirement.

---

[58] FTC Act § 5(a), 15 U.S.C. § 45(a)(1).
https://www.law.cornell.edu/uscode/text/15/45.
[59] While the FTC's authority comes from the FTC Act and the specified power over "unfair" or "deceptive" trade practices, you will not find the words "privacy" or "cybersecurity" anywhere in the FTC Act. The FTC's authority on these areas has been challenged and is far from absolute. If your organization is in a specific sector, see the later subsection because there may be a federal law that applies on cyber. And don't forget state laws.

Now New York has a requirement for reasonable cybersecurity, incident response, and data breach notification to state government agencies and affected parties. The SHIELD Act is found within the New York State General Business Law ("GBL" or "GBS") §899-aa and §899-bb.[60]

Your State

Check your state's laws regarding:

- Data breach reporting and notification (every state has such a law)
- Cybersecurity requirements (many states have such a law)
- Privacy requirements (some states have such a law).

Financial sector

The financial sector is heavily regulated on many topics including cybersecurity to ensure the safety and soundness of a financial institution, protect consumers and prevent cybercrime. This regulation is through many federal laws, regulations, and regulators. States have their rules too.

Federal rules to consider include:

- The Gramm-Leach-Bliley Act (GLBA) (also known as the Financial Services Modernization Act of 1999) and related regulations on privacy and cybersecurity.
- The Sarbanes-Oxley Act of 2002 (SOX) requires publicly traded companies to have proper internal control structures in place including with their information systems.
- The Federal Financial Institutions Examination Council (FFIEC) is a group of federal financial regulators that establishes common federal standards information technology and cybersecurity (among other areas).

Here in New York (where we call ourselves the financial capital of the world) there is a state cybersecurity regulation from the New York State

---

[60] NY GBL § 899-aa Notification; person without valid authorization has acquired private information,
https://www.nysenate.gov/legislation/laws/GBS/899-AA
NY GBL § 899-bb Data security protections,
https://www.nysenate.gov/legislation/laws/GBS/899-BB
NY GBL § 399H, Disposal of records containing personal identifying information, https://www.nysenate.gov/legislation/laws/GBS/399-H

Department of Financial Services (DFS), which is DFS Rule 500, Cybersecurity Requirements for Financial Services Companies.[61]

Health sector

The health sector needs to comply with laws and regulations to protect patient health information and other private information, and to ensure our health sector is protected from cyberattack and natural disaster. The main rules are laid out in Health Insurance Portability and Accountability Act (HIPAA). This law is periodically amended, including in 2009 by the by the Health Information Technology for Economic and Clinical Health Act (HITECH).

HIPAA empowers the U.S. Department of Health and Human Services (HHS) to create rules and regulations in accordance with the law. They created rules (regulations) regarding cybersecurity, privacy, and breach notification.[62]

As always, compliance should start with good cybersecurity, cybercrime protection, and privacy practices. Then, organizations can analyze details of these requirements.

Finding more on specific laws

Much more detail is on my website, and even more authoritative is from the websites of the enforcers of a particular cybersecurity or privacy law. The regulators often put out good guidance on how to comply with the rules.

19.7 References and additional reading

- Cyberlaw,
  https://johnbandler.com/cyberlaw/
- Cybersecurity laws 1,
  https://johnbandler.com/cybersecurity-laws-and-regulations-1/
- Cybersecurity laws 2,
  https://johnbandler.com/cybersecurity-laws-and-regulations-2/

---

[61] NYS DFS Rule 500 is found at 23 NY Codes, Rules and Regulations (NYCRR) Part 500, https://www.law.cornell.edu/regulations/new-york/title-23/chapter-I/part-500

[62] The bulk of these HIPAA related regulations are found in the code of federal regulations (CFR) within 45 CFR Part 164, https://www.law.cornell.edu/cfr/text/45/part-164

- Cyberlaw things to know,
  https://johnbandler.com/things-to-know-cyberlaw/
- Federal Trade Commission (FTC) law and information
  - FTC Act § 5(a), 15 U.S.C. § 45(a)(1),
    https://www.law.cornell.edu/uscode/text/15/45
  - https://www.ftc.gov/tips-advice/business-center/privacy-and-security
  - https://www.ftc.gov/about-ftc/what-we-do/enforcement-authority
- Financial sector cyber laws,
  https://johnbandler.com/financial-sector-cyber-laws-regulations/
- Health sector cyber laws,
  https://johnbandler.com/health-sector-laws-and-regulations/
- Cybersecurity articles
  - Introduction to cybersecurity,
    https://johnbandler.com/introduction-cybersecurity-information-security/
  - Cybersecurity tips, https://johnbandler.com/cybersecurity-tips-from-john-bandler/
  - Priority cybercrime threats, https://johnbandler.com/priority-cybercrime-threats/
- Books
  - Cybersecurity for the Home and Office
  - Cybercrime Investigations (includes chapters on criminal laws, civil laws, and international law)

20

Cybersecurity external guidance

In this chapter:

- What is a cybersecurity framework
- From who
- For who
- Learn the names of some common frameworks
- NIST Cybersecurity Framework (CSF)

➔ ➔ ➔ ➔ ➔ ➔ ➔ ➔ ➔ ➔ ➔ ➔ ➔ ➔ ➔ ➔

▶▶❙ Skippable if your project does not involve cybersecurity.

20.1. What is a cybersecurity framework

Simply put, a cybersecurity framework is a structured set of best practices to help manage an organization's cybersecurity.

There are many useful best practices for cybersecurity to help organizations with the complex task of managing and securing their information assets.[63]

These cybersecurity frameworks are considered external guidance within the context of this book and policy work—voluntary and not mandatory. Organizations may choose to follow, adapt, or disregard these frameworks.[64]

---

[63] Remember that cybersecurity is a subset of information security, though many use the terms interchangeably.

[64] In contrast, if a cybersecurity law applies to an organization, that is a mandatory external rule. The organization would not be able to simply disregard or "adapt" the law but must abide by it. Compare also that some cybersecurity

Cybersecurity is complicated so we cannot expect every organization to reinvent the wheel as they secure themselves.[65] On the one hand, every organization is different so one size does not fit all. On the other hand, the practice of effective cybersecurity is well understood and with many resources available.

20.2 Who creates these frameworks?

Anyone can create frameworks or other guidance. Many frameworks are written by excellent teams of smart people in reputable organizations.

Some come from government, such as the National Institute of Standards and Technology (NIST), an agency of the U.S. Department of Commerce. The NIST frameworks are created and maintained by qualified people in our government, paid for with federal tax dollars, and made publicly available at no cost and with no license agreement. It's a great deal so NIST should be a first stop for any complex framework, standard, or similar type of publications.

Some frameworks come from for-profit or not-for-profit organizations.[66] Some may be available for easy inspection and review, others may require a fee or membership. Occasionally licensing agreements (a contract) are involved to protect their intellectual property and their business models.

I created a cybersecurity framework. It is simple and free and valuable and can get any organization started (as we cover in the next chapter).

Some of the other frameworks can be complex and well beyond what the average person can understand. This can make them too complex for most small organizations. The concept of my framework is

---

laws have a provision to presume compliance with the law if the organization is properly following a framework.

Further, there might be circumstances where a "voluntary" framework becomes mandatory thanks to a contract or other requirement. For example, a contract to use a payment card processing system might requires compliance with the PCI-DSS standards which can be considered a framework.

[65] Similarly, builders and mechanics consult best practices as well. An auto mechanic doing a complicated repair on your car may consult a manual that tells them the steps to complete the repair. An architect or builder uses tools to plan their creation. A cybersecurity framework is similar.

[66] Some may even be a mix of for-profit and non-profit components.

understandable in thirty seconds, with the ability to layer in more detail later.

20.3 Who are the frameworks for?

All of the frameworks (except mine) are geared for readers with a high degree of technology and information security knowledge, meaning they are primarily for organizations with sufficient information security programs and staff. They can be too technical for most laypersons to understand, and too complex for most smaller and mid-sized organizations to implement.

Some framework developers have created guides to help small and mid-sized organizations handle some of the basics. The very recent update to the NIST Cybersecurity Framework improves its accessibility to small and medium sized organizations.

20.4 A quick listing of cybersecurity frameworks

The following lists well regarded cybersecurity frameworks. The point is not to memorize them but be familiar with the names and where you can learn more about each.

- Bandler's Four Pillars of Cybersecurity (more next chapter)
- Critical Security Controls (CSC) from the Center for Internet Security (CIS) (now at 18 CSC, previously was 20)
- Frameworks from National Institute of Standards and Technology (NIST)
  - NIST Cybersecurity Framework (CSF) v 2.0, (a new release, see the next section)
  - NIST SP 800-53 Rev 5: NIST Special Publication 800-53, Security and Privacy Controls for Federal Information Systems and Organizations
  - NIST SP 800-171 Rev. 2, Protecting Controlled Unclassified Information in Nonfederal Systems and Organizations
- Cybersecurity Performance Goals (CPGs) from CISA (in coordination with NIST)
- International Organization for Standardization (ISO) 27001 (27000 series) standard for Information Security Management Systems (ISMS). This framework comes with an industry of independent third-party certification services. The 27000 series is the successor to the ISO 17799 standard)

- COBIT from ISACA
  COBIT = Control Objectives for Information and Related
  Technology
  ISACA = Previously known as the Information Systems Audit
  and Control Association, now just "ISACA"
- AICPA SSAE 18 SOC 2 & SOC 3 (ability for third party
  attestation services)
  AICPA = American Institute of Certified Public Accountants
  SSAE = Statement of Standards for Attestation Engagement
  SOC = Service and Organization Controls
  This is found in the AICPA 2017 Trust Services Criteria for
  Security, Availability, Processing Integrity, Confidentiality, and
  Privacy.
  These also have an industry of third-party attestation services.
- PCI-DSS Payment Card Industry (PCI) Data Security Standard
  (DSS) (security for credit and debit cards and more, and may be
  required by contract for merchants)
- NERC CIP North American Electric Reliability Corporation
  (NERC) Critical Infrastructure Protection (CIP) Cybersecurity
  Standards
- HITRUST Common Security Framework (CSF) (framework and
  ability for third party attestation services)
- Cybersecurity Maturity Model Certification (CMMC) from
  Department of Defense (DOD)

There are more!

Each framework above sets forth a process and method to protect
information systems and all the complexities that come with that. While
they have similarities they are also all different, organized differently,
use different terminology, and may have different priorities.

You can learn more about each from the organization that puts forth the
framework, and my site has a brief summary of most of them.

20.5 NIST CSF

The NIST Cybersecurity Framework (CSF) version 2.0 was released on
February 26, 2024.[67] It replaces version 1.1 which had an official title
"Framework for Improving Critical Infrastructure Cybersecurity" and

---

[67] Just as I was doing the final proofreading on this book!

was released April 2018. Version 2 does away with that clunky official title, so now it is both officially and informally the Cybersecurity Framework (CSF).

The NIST CSF is valuable cybersecurity guidance, free to access and use with just the click of a mouse, with no registration, no fee, and no licensing agreement. It was created and updated by smart people with a rigorous process, paid for with U.S. tax dollars. Organizations should take advantage of it.

Version 2 is much more accessible than the prior version and has multiple quick start guides. Still, it still may be too technical for many individuals to understand, and for many smaller and mid-sized organizations to implement.

The NIST CSF has some heft to it, between its own page and word count, and all the accompanying documents that come along with it. It is a tough read so some readers would need to research many of the terms and might not understand it. In addition, there are many other documents and quick start guides and those can take time to digest. If an organization is going to claim that they follow the NIST CSF, the first hurdle is having someone within the organization who has read and understands the NIST CSF. Most organizations do not have such a person.

The NIST CSF v. 2.0 is organized into six main "functions" of:

- Govern
- Identify
- Protect
- Detect
- Respond
- Recover.

The framework recognizes the effort of cybersecurity through these six functions in an ongoing, cyclical process. These functions are further subdivided into categories, and they are laid out below:

- Govern (GV)
    - Organizational Context (GV.OC)
    - Risk Management Strategy (GV.RM)
    - Roles, Responsibilities, and Authorities (GV.RR)
    - Policy (GV.PO)
    - Oversight (GV.OV)
    - Cybersecurity Supply Chain Risk Management (GV.SC)

- Identify (ID)
  - o Asset Management (ID.AM)
  - o Risk Assessment (ID.RA)
  - o Improvement (ID.IM)
- Protect (PR)
  - o Identity Management, Authentication and Access Control (PR.AA)
  - o Awareness and Training (PR.AT)
  - o Data Security (PR.DS)
  - o Platform Security (PR.PS)
  - o Technology Infrastructure Resilience (PR.IR)
- Detect (DE)
  - o Continuous Monitoring (DE.CM)
  - o Adverse Event Analysis (DE.AE)
- Respond (RS)
  - o Incident Management (RS.MA)
  - o Incident Analysis (RS.AN)
  - o Incident Response Reporting and Communication (RS.CO)
  - o Incident Mitigation (RS.MI)
- Recover (RC)
  - o Incident Recovery Plan Execution (RC.RP)
  - o Incident Recovery Communication (RC.CO).

CSF v.2.0 added the function of "govern", a welcome addition, since management and governance are an essential part of cybersecurity. There is a specific category of "policy" (though their exact definition of policy may be different from ours). As we know from this book, policy work is an essential part of governance.

This is the NIST CSF's method for organizing the process of cybersecurity, and remember that other frameworks do it differently, with different categories and terminology.

If you find the NIST terminology above confusing, or read the actual framework and find that confusing, then please read the next chapter and see how the Four Pillars of Cybersecurity compares for you.

20.6 References and additional reading

- Cybersecurity frameworks and guidance, https://johnbandler.com/cybersecurity-frameworks-and-guidance/

- NIST cybersecurity framework, https://johnbandler.com/nist-cybersecurity-framework/
- Four Pillars of Cybersecurity, see next chapter.
- NIST Cybersecurity Framework landing page, https://www.nist.gov/cyberframework

John Bandler

21

The Four Pillars of Cybersecurity

(more cybersecurity external guidance)

In this chapter:

- Four Pillars of Cybersecurity
    - o   Improve **knowledge** and awareness
    - o   Secure computer **devices**
    - o   Secure **data**, applications and accounts
    - o   Secure **networks** and internet usage
- Repeat

➔ ➔ ➔ ➔ ➔ ➔ ➔ ➔ ➔ ➔ ➔ ➔ ➔ ➔ ➔ ➔

⏭ Skippable if your project has nothing to do with cybersecurity
⏭ Skippable if you already adopted an information security framework

The Four Pillars in a nutshell

My Four Pillars of Cybersecurity is a cybersecurity framework anyone can understand. It is a great starting point for individuals, small and mid-sized organizations looking for cybersecurity plan and practice guidance.

It is also a helpful tool for individuals in larger organizations to better comprehend the cybersecurity framework their organization has adopted.

If an organization using the Four Pillars framework increases in size and maturity to the point where it requires a more complex framework, they simply begin a transition by supplementing with more complex and detailed guidance, such as the NIST Cybersecurity Framework, or the CIS 18 Critical Security Controls.

The four pillars of cybersecurity are:

1. Improve knowledge and awareness
   - To improve decision making by everyone from the CEO to newest hire.
     Learn about cybercrime threats, information security, technology, and legal requirements
2. Secure computing devices
3. Secure data
4. Secure networks and use of the Internet

Repeat! It's a continual process of improvement.

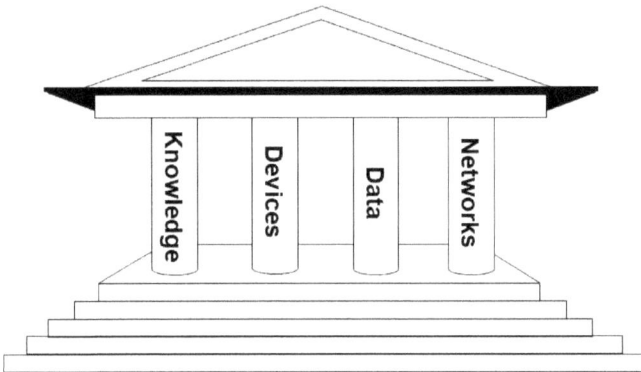

Bandler's Four Pillars of Cybersecurity

The allure of this conceptual framework is its simplicity and efficiency. Every person, from the newest hire to the head of the organization, from the luddite to the IT professional, can comprehend it.

That is important because cybersecurity is for everyone, from end users to the leaders who make important decisions about information assets. It focuses on four key areas and emphasizes continual and cyclical improvement. Let's review each pillar.

1. Knowledge and awareness

Every person needs a degree of knowledge and awareness to make good decisions about technology, cybersecurity, and cybercrime. The employee's lack of knowledge might result in a devastating cybercrime. The organization leader's lack of knowledge might result in disastrous decisions regarding information technology and security.

Imagine trying to secure your home without knowing how a door operates, or how to engage the lock. Imagine trying to drive a car safely without understanding basic principles of how a car works, rules of the road, or the simple rules of nature like "slippery when wet".

Knowledge and awareness of cybersecurity should extend to:

- Legal requirements.
- Organization internal rules (including written policies, procedures, and more).
- Cybercrime threats, including:
  - Email based funds transfer frauds ("business email compromise" and "CEO Fraud")
  - Malware, including ransomware
  - Data breaches and data theft
  - Social engineering (con artistry) and similar threats aimed at people
  - Phishing
  - Identity theft
- Privacy threats.
- Basic information security principles.
- How computers work.
- How networks and the internet work.
- How to implement basic security measures.
- Risk management, decision making, and making good security decisions.
- The importance of cybersecurity in the home, and how security at work and home are interrelated.
- How working remotely creates and increases security risks.

2. Protect computing devices

Computing devices need to be secured. This includes smartphones, tablets, laptops, desktops, servers, networking devices, printers and more. This means:

- Inventory all devices and develop a process for bringing them into service securely (commissioning) and taking them out of service securely when no longer needed (decommissioning).
- Ensure physical security and control over these devices. Devices need to be protected from loss, damage, or theft.
- Configure devices properly.
- Update (patch) of devices.

- Protect against malware.
- Protect against intrusion.
- Control access.
- Periodic review of security and privacy settings.

3. Protect data and online accounts and applications

Data needs to be protected from breach and data needs to be available when needed. Certain data breaches could trigger reporting requirements and halt business operations.

This means:

- Inventory data (to a reasonable degree of detail).
- Inventory applications (to a reasonable degree of detail).
- Inventory cloud-based services and apps (to a reasonable degree of detail).
- Secure cloud accounts properly with complex, unique passwords, and a second factor of authentication (multi-factor authentication, MFA, or 2FA).
- Control access to data.
- Secure data in a manner commensurate with its sensitivity.
- Encrypt certain data as warranted.
- Delete unneeded data.
- Back up data regularly and securely.

4. Protect networks and safe use of the internet

Data is constantly flowing between our internal devices and through the internet. Key concepts include:

- Inventory network hardware and physically secure it.
- Securely configure routers and switches.
- Use unique (and non-default) passwords.
- Keep devices patched (updated).
- Disable unneeded features.
- Encrypt Wi-Fi networks and require a strong password to join. Change this password periodically.
- Consider intrusion prevention and monitoring.
- Understand the route that data takes as it flows.
- Avoid or minimize the use of public networks.
- Encrypt data in transit whenever practical.
- Encrypt certain data at the file level for transmittal.

Repeat (continually improve)

Cybersecurity is never "done" so we take small continual steps and work to continually improve security and the strength of each of the four pillars.

Four Pillars as a simple entry point for organizations and people

The Four Pillars is perfect for individuals, small organizations, and many medium sized organizations. It is also a helpful tool for individuals in larger organizations to better understand the more complex cybersecurity framework their organization has adopted.

As mentioned, there are many other cybersecurity frameworks which are excellent and more detailed, but they are geared for readers and organizations with a higher degree of cybersecurity knowledge and program maturity.

Four Pillars is defensible and extensible

The Four Pillars of Cybersecurity is defensible and comprehensible for every organization employee.

It can be supplemented and extended with other guidance, including from NIST and other reputable organizations. These can add greater detail and organizations can adopt more complex frameworks as they increase in size and maturity.

It is simple for the organization to begin a transition by supplementing with more complex and detailed guidance, such as the NIST Cybersecurity Framework (CSF), or the CIS Eighteen Critical Security Controls. Even as maturation takes place the Four Pillars remains helpful because cybersecurity is a responsibility of every employee, and not every employee can be a cybersecurity professional with the ability to understand the more complex frameworks.

You can craft a cybersecurity policy from it – or use mine

The Four Pillars of Cybersecurity is suitable for adapting to an organization's written cybersecurity policy. In fact, I have done that for you with my free policy.

References and additional reading

- Four Pillars of Cybersecurity,
  https://johnbandler.com/bandlers-four-pillars-of-cybersecurity/
- Cybersecurity Tips,
  https://johnbandler.com/cybersecurity-tips-from-john-bandler/
- Free Cybersecurity Policy,
  https://johnbandler.com/cybersecurity-policy-free-version/

Four Pillars of Cybersecurity

Cybersecurity Tips

Free cybersecurity policy

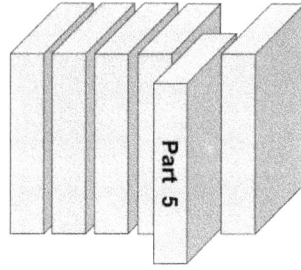

Part 5

Use and maintain
your new policies

The house is built. Now we need to live in it and maintain it.

When does the boiler need to be serviced, when does the house need paint or caulk, when do we need to do a small or major renovation?

22

Use and maintain your new policies

Review and update them

In this chapter:

- Use and maintain
- Review
- Update
- Start a new project

22.1 Use and Maintain

We have new governance documents in place—or a new version of an existing document—now it is time to use and maintain them.

They are not shelfware, but living documents to be used, reviewed, and updated as needed. If the documents are not being used or followed or if they become out of date, then management needs to identify that and address the situation.

By continually updating the documents they will remain useful, instead of becoming obsolete and eventually requiring a large project to get them back to viability.

In other words, small steps and small improvements keep you on track and current. While you do this, you are keeping the organization's focus on important issues of mission, action, and compliance. If you let the documents gather dust, they will become out of date and obsolete in short order.

22.2 Review

Review your policies and procedures. Simple, right?

Remember that "review" is the "R" in ENTER, Five Steps for Governance Documents.[68]

Your review should include evaluating and looking for issues or changes in any of the Five Components for Policy work:

- External rules
- Mission
- Practice
- External guidance
- Internal rules (e.g., this and other governance documents).

Governance document review should be done:

- Continually (easy to say, harder to do)
- Annually (a good rule to have)
- As circumstances require (another good rule to have).

Continual review

Review can be conducted continually, as operations identify issues, or as circumstances change with the business, laws, or best practices. As issues arise, the policy manager can create a list of notes and action items, to be addressed at the annual review. Questions can arise any time an employee consults the document, a new hire asks a question, or the organization encounters a situation.

Annual review

At a minimum, review should be conducted annually. Put this in the calendar and on the agenda of any relevant meetings.

If you fail to review your policies every year, you risk them becoming obsolete and unworkable, and then you will find yourself in a position where you need to perform a major policy project.[69]

---

[68] As covered previously, ENTER stands for:
    Evaluate circumstances and documents
    Newly create or update documents
    Train
    Ensure practice follows policy
    Review and update periodically.
[69] Stain your deck every year and it will last a long time. Forget to stain it and you will need to replace it eventually. Check your house exterior and if you see

When circumstances require

Conduct a review when circumstances require. These circumstances could include:

- Organization sale, investment, merger, etc.
- Changes in law
- Changes in technology or way of doing business, methods of providing goods or services
- Events or actions that may need to be addressed in policies
  - Regular organization or employee action that is not in compliance with:
    - Existing policy
    - External rules
    - Mission
  - Employee action or misconduct occurs that should have been prohibited by policy
  - Regulatory actions or lawsuits identifying weakness in policies or practices
  - Current events that identify gaps or weaknesses in policies or practices
- Questions from employees, managers, third-parties that identify issues in the current policies
  - A new employee who asks what something means, and managers don't know how to answer
  - Employees or managers who identify confusing language or ways the language or rules could be improved
  - Auditor questions
  - Third-party review questions.

This review can be simple or complex, including one or more of the following:

- Read-through by the person or people in charge of implementing and supervising the document.
- Email to the stakeholders asking them to review and reply with any suggestions or comments.

---

the paint peeling, if you see some caulk is needed, identify it, and schedule the work.

Dear [stakeholder people], we are doing our annual review of the XYZ policy. Please review it and let me know if you have suggestions to improve it.

- Formal agenda item with appropriate due diligence from organizational units responsible for the document.

Whatever the level of detail, this review should be documented in some fashion, even with a simple email. For example:

Dear [supervisor person],

I did our annual review of the XYZ policy and do not think it needs any immediate changes. Perhaps for next year we should think about issue ABC since I think there will be some new laws coming.

As you review, consider training, including for new hires, and refresher training for existing employees. If updates are a regular occurrence, training on the update can be combined with refresher training.

Also consider other documents that might conflict or need updating. If you have a new document that is the product of careful thought, it is worth examining if there are other documents that conflict with it and need to be updated or deprecated (rendered obsolete).

22.3 Update if needed

If the review indicates that updates are needed, then perform that update.

The update can be minor or major.

With our internal rules platform analogy, we could think of this update as:

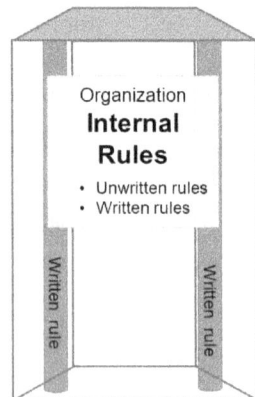

Organization
Internal Rules
- Unwritten rules
- Written rules

Written rule

Written rule

Internal Rules Platform cross section

- A coat of paint on the faces of the platform
- Structural work on the faces to strengthen or repair them
- Adding pillars
- Reinforcing or rebuilding pillars
- Changing the overall platform height so it aligns better with:
  - External rules
  - Mission.

If governance documents are continually reviewed and updated then they will grow and evolve with the organization.

By doing this regularly, the organization stays efficient and in compliance, and individuals remain familiar with all the issues and written rules. Policy documents will never be perfect or "done", but this keeps important issues front and center.

22.4 Start a new project?

Is an update just an "update" or a "project"?

What constitutes a "project" will depend on your organization and involves a matter of degree and how it is articulated.[70]

An update could be considered a project or a mini project, but there might be organizational reasons not to call it this.

If certain organization "projects" need certain approvals, remember that conducting a regular policy review and a minor update should not require a specific approval. After all, if the policy says it needs to be reviewed annually then that review is already explicitly approved and mandated by the organization (even if external budget is not explicitly approved). If the review indicates that updates are needed, then the update is needed.

In other words, policy managers should not need to seek and obtain supervisor approval to review a policy. Such review should already by part and parcel of the existing policy.

If updates have been done periodically, and there have not been major changes in the organization or laws, then you should not need a major project. The people and concepts and practices should be largely in place, and you are on track for smooth and efficient updates.

If your policy documents have become hopelessly obsolete, and it is unclear who oversees them or what changes should be made, then a greater degree of project formality may be needed. You must determine who should be involved, the process, the desired product and gaps you are closing. If you perform regular reviews and updates, you can largely avoid this state of uncertainty.

---

[70] Some might dismissively say it is just a matter of "semantics", but when we are dealing with policies, procedures, and a book on it, everything involves semantics! Semantics is "the branch of linguistics and logic concerned with meaning." Oxford Languages Dictionary via Google.
Also *see* https://en.wikipedia.org/wiki/Semantics.

A goal of having created a quality governance document in the first place is that it can grow and evolve with your organization. You will not need a major document project on this topic unless the organization experiences a merger or sale and adaptation is needed to accommodate organization changes.

The organization may see other topic areas where this exact project process can be utilized to improve those areas.

22.5 References and additional reading

- Use and maintain your policies, https://johnbandler.com/use-maintain-policies/

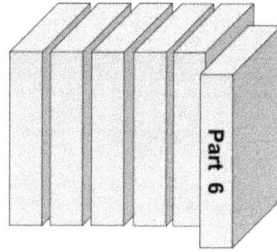

Part 6

Conclusion
and
Resources

"Appendix"

- Conclusion
- Glossary
- References and additional reading
- Policy checklist
- Quick start guide
- My journey to write the book
- List of diagrams
- Index

23

Conclusion

In this chapter:

- Wrap it up!

Did you skip to here just to see how the story ended?

It ends with solid governance documents built through a solid process that improved both the organization and the individuals who worked on it.

Or did you read this book all the way through and make it to the end here? If so, I hope the book was an informative and pleasant read and will remain a helpful reference and resource. Feel free to reach out and connect or even provide kind and constructive notes about how I can make it better for the next edition.

Every person and situation is different, so what is helpful information or pleasant style for some may land differently for others. It helps me to hear what readers think as I plan the next edition.

Interested in more books of this type? My "to do" list includes books on:

- Introduction to Law
- Cyberlaw
- Cybersecurity
- Privacy.

Thank you for getting to here.

More resources follow.

John Bandler

24

Glossary

Words mean different things to different people, with often fascinating and sometimes confounding results.

This is what these words mean to me for the purpose of this book and in the simplest of fashions.

I'm not trying to be fancy or hyper-technical and I'm not trying to lawyer it up with legalese. I simplify and try provide information in a simple format. If you need greater detail or precision, you might find it in the book as all these terms are indexed. My website might have information too.

Consult other reliable sources too. Many people have spent a great deal of time defining terms. Semantics matters and words have different meanings depending on the individual issuing or receiving them.

If a law or regulation defines a term, that has legal significance for compliance purposes. Frameworks define terms for the purpose of that body of work. Consider the context in which you use a word.

Appendix: Sort of what I call Part 6 since it is a common term. But I am not a fan of it because the human appendix is a totally unnecessary organ that sometimes causes a pain, whereas Part 6 is necessary and helpful information and causes no pain.

Backwards planning: Knowing when and where you need to be as a final deadline, then looking backwards from there to determine what needs to be done to get there.

Compliance: The process of complying with external rules (laws and regulations and other legal requirements), as well as compliance with internal rules (policies and procedures).

Component: A generic term to indicate a part of a whole, e.g., a component such as a platform or a cloud. See Five Components for Policy Work.

Cyber: A much overused term that is used alone and in combination with almost every other dictionary term. It mostly means related to computers, networks, and the Internet.

Cybercrime: Cyber + crime. When someone violates a criminal statute using computers and the internet. Most cybercrime is ultimately about theft but there are many typologies and also other motives.

Cyberlaw: Cyber + law. The areas of law relating to computers and the internet, including areas of criminal law, cybersecurity, privacy, nation-state conflict, and more.

Cybersecurity: Cyber + security. The process of securing digital information (and information assets while we are at it) and protecting from cybercrime. In practical terms, think of it being the same as information security. The objectives of cybersecurity are confidentiality, integrity, and availability (CIA) of digital assets.

Decision making: The process of making choices, especially effective ones. Hopefully all reasonable options were considered and there was a reasonable process to consider facts and risks, and a reasonable decision was reached.

Easter Egg: A surprise or hidden joke. If I put something in this book that has nothing to do with policies or if I make a ridiculous joke, it is probably an Easter Egg. If you find a typo please consider it a deliberate Easter Egg (but also please let me know so I can fix it).

Evangelizing: A term I used to use more to denote sharing knowledge, teaching, and persuading about the best course of action for the organization. But it is a term with differing perceptions. "Persuading", "informing" or "gaining consensus" might be better terms.

External guidance: Best practices, expert advice, or anything from outside the organization that the organization could use or adapt to guide its policy or practice. One of the Five Components for Policy Work.

External rule: A law, statute, regulation, court decision or legally binding contract. One of the Five Components for Policy Work.

Five Components for Policy Work: A concept from John Bandler applicable for policies and management that focus on external rules, internal rules, practice, mission, and external guidance.

Four Pillars of Cybersecurity: A concept (framework) from John Bandler for organizing cybersecurity that everyone can understand, which involves building people's knowledge and awareness, securing devices, secure data, and secure networks. Repeat and keep improving.

Glossary: You're in the glossary now. If you need more explaining, you may need to hire someone to do your policy work for you. Seriously though, a glossary is just one person's definition of terms.

Governance: Governance is basically just management. The process or act of overseeing or managing.

Governance documents: Documents from the organization that tell the organization and people within it what to do. Examples include policies and procedures, and also bylaws, articles of incorporation, standards, handbooks, etc. This book is all about governance documents.

Governance, risk, and compliance (GRC): A term where these three items are often grouped together to comply with external rules (compliance), address risks, and also how the organization is managed.

Information assets: Assets of an organization relating to information systems, including people, computer devices, data, networks and communication methods.

Information governance: The process of managing information assets and information systems.

Information security: Similar to cybersecurity, but it has been around longer and could include non-cyber information (paper, verbal statements, etc.). For practical convenience think of it being the same as cybersecurity. The objectives of information security are confidentiality, integrity, and availability (CIA) of information assets.

Internal rules: Within the Five Components for Policy Work, internal rules are those made by the organization, including verbal, written, policies, procedures, etc. This book is all about internal rules.

Johnbandler.com: The domain name for a website you will really enjoy. Please give me some views, clicks, and shares.

Law: A vast area of government rules for conduct and a process for resolving disputes. Hard to explain in a glossary, maybe I need to write a book on it. Or if an online course might interest you, share a kind word and I might be inclined to give you a coupon code to my Udemy course.

Management: The process of managing (governing or directing) an organization. E.g., good management is what we strive for.

Operations: Ongoing and repetitive tasks that produce the same outcome every time they are performed. Compare this to a project.

Organization: An entity of some sort, whether for-profit business, non-profit organization, or government agency or unit. This is my catch-all term because other words like "business", "corporation", are more specific and might exclude certain organizations.

People: Humans, or Homo Sapiens, indisputably the most difficult and destructive of all species on our planet, even the universe. Also the only species that writes policies and procedures, and (occasionally) reads them.

Pillars: An upright column, usually supporting something else. One of my metaphors of choice. See the Four Pillars of Cybersecurity and the internal rules platform (which may have pillars inside it).

Platforms: A structure you could stand or walk on. Another metaphor of choice. See for example the Three Platforms to Connect for Compliance, and the Four Platforms.

Policy: A term used two ways in this book.

> **Policy** as a specific type of document: A governance document that is general and of higher authority and should not need to be changed frequently. Compare with standards and procedures which are sequentially lower level and more detail.

> **Policy** as a generic term, e.g., policies, "policy-work". A more general way to describe governance documents in general, to avoid having to say, "governance documents", "policies and procedures", or "policies and procedures and other governance documents".

> Remember this term could have alternate meanings depending on context and your organization.

Portfolio: A group of multiple projects, programs and operations. A person might manage a portfolio of stuff that includes all of these things.

Practice (action). What you do. Your practices. The actions and practices of the organization.

Privacy: "The right to be let alone" and a growing area of law and compliance and policy regarding consumer data. Privacy also includes a cybersecurity component.

Procedure: A governance document that is a step-by step instruction on how to accomplish a task. It has many details and might need to be updated frequently.

Program: A group that could include multiple projects with a common goal, probably with a program manager to oversee them.

Project: A finite and limited work endeavor with a planned and defined start, ending, scope, and a unique product, service, or result. For example, a document project to create or update a policy or procedure. Compare with operations which is ongoing and without a start or planned end.

Project management: The process of managing a project, from planning, start, to end. Projects should be managed well!

Pyramid (as in rules pyramid): A governance document metaphor that depicts policies, standards, and procedures. I am not a fan of it and I like the rules platform metaphor instead.

Risk: A downside, a "con", a potential harm that could occur because of a threat. We also factor in the probability, potential frequency, and magnitude of that harm.

Risk management: The process of managing risks. Risks should be managed reasonably and diligently. Still, we can't eliminate all risks. Take a look at "decision making" also because it is related.

Rules: A rule or an instruction. Rules could be written or unwritten. Organizations need rules, governments create rules too. See Internal rules and External rules.

Scope creep: When the original scope keeps creeping little by little until it is much larger than was anticipated. For example, if your planned four-page policy document now is a fifty page behemoth, the scope might have crept.

Socializing: A term I used once upon a time about getting people accustomed to a concept or document. Then I read somewhere it can be considered confusing and annoying business speak, so perhaps "gaining consensus", "informing" or "persuading" are better terms.

Training: A process, whether formal or informal, of getting employees to learn something helpful and positive.

Version control: A process of keeping track of a version of a document, with two main instances (1) organization approved versions over time and (2) document draft versions during a governance document project.

25

References and additional reading

This is a consolidated list of references and additional reading.

Remember that at the end of most chapters there are references listed pertaining to that chapter.

The landing pages may be updated from time to time.

Find my policy reference list online

Policy and Procedure References,
https://johnbandler.com/policy-and-procedure-references/

Policy and Procedure Reference Details,
https://johnbandler.com/policy-and-procedure-reference-details/

General policy resources

JohnBandler.com (my website)

John Bandler, Policies and Procedures for Your Organization: Build solid governance documents on any topic ... including cybersecurity (John Bandler, 2024) (This Book!) [71]

---

[71] Is it even possible (or legal) to use this book as a reference for itself? I am testing the limits. It keeps this list complete and if someone copies out these references for future use, they will not forget about the book.

John Bandler, Corporate Security Policies, online learning path hosted by Infosec Skills, a Cengage company. Available at, https://www.infosecinstitute.com/skills/learning-paths/corporate-security-policies/

Other works

John Bandler, Cybersecurity for the Home and Office: The Lawyer's Guide to Taking Charge of Your Own Information Security (American Bar Association, 2017).[72]

John Bandler and Antonia Merzon, Cybercrime Investigations: A Comprehensive Resource for Everyone (CRC Press, 2020).[73]

The Five Components for Policy Work resources

Five Components for Policy Work, https://johnbandler.com/five-components-for-policy-work/

Three Platforms to Connect for Compliance, https://johnbandler.com/bandlers-three-platforms-to-connect/

Fourth Platform to Connect, https://johnbandler.com/bandlers-fourth-platform-to-connect/

ENTER: Five Steps for Governance Documents, https://johnbandler.com/enter-five-steps-for-governance-documents/

Internal Rules, https://johnbandler.com/internal-rules/

External Rules, https://johnbandler.com/external-rules/

External Guidance, https://johnbandler.com/external-guidance/

Practice (action), https://johnbandler.com/practice-action/

Mission and Business Goals, https://johnbandler.com/business-needs-and-mission/

---

[72] My first book and the debut of the Four Pillars of Cybersecurity. More information at link including the acknowledgements to the many who helped with it. You don't need to buy the book, just know I wrote it and it influenced this. https://johnbandler.com/cybersecurity-for-the-home-and-office/

[73] My second book, with a co-author who also put prodigious work into it. It discusses many important topics. Again, you don't have to buy it, just know I wrote it and it influenced this. https://johnbandler.com/cybercrime-investigations/

Law resources

Rules, https://johnbandler.com/rules/

Law, https://johnbandler.com/law/

Cyberlaw, https://johnbandler.com/cyberlaw/

Contract law, https://johnbandler.com/contract-law/

Negligence law, https://johnbandler.com/negligence-law/

Privacy, https://johnbandler.com/privacy/

Criminal law, https://johnbandler.com/criminal-law/

Cybersecurity Laws and Regulations 1, https://johnbandler.com/cybersecurity-laws-and-regulations-1/

Cybersecurity Laws and Regulations Part 2, https://johnbandler.com/cybersecurity-laws-and-regulations-2/

Health Sector Laws and Regulations, https://johnbandler.com/health-sector-laws-and-regulations/

Financial Sector Cyber Laws and Regulations, https://johnbandler.com/financial-sector-cyber-laws-regulations/

Books on policies and procedures as a general matter (not focused on cybersecurity)[74]

Campbell, Nancy, Writing Effective Policies and Procedures: A Step-by-Step Resource for Clear Communication (AMACOM, 1998)

Brumby, Kirsten, How to Write Effective Policies and Procedures: The System that Makes the Process of Developing Policies and Procedures Easy (Mind Potential Publishing, 2021)

Peabody, Larry, How to Write Policies, Procedures & Task Outlines: Sending Clear Signals in Written Directions (Writing Services, 2006)

---

[74] By listing these books, I am not necessarily recommending that you purchase them and you should evaluate price. Many of these books may be out of print, prices may fluctuate and they may not be cost effective for purchase. For example, there are books I purchased for about $10 and were a good value at that price, but Amazon now lists them at over $100 (no longer a good value).

I've read others but will not list them here. Have a book to suggest? Let me know.

Books on policies and procedures for information security, cybersecurity, data security, information technology[75]

Raggad, Bel G, Information Security Management, Concepts and Practice (CRC Press, 2010)[76]

Landoll, Douglas J, Information Security Policies, Procedures, and Standards: A Practitioner's Reference (Auerbach Publications, 2020)

Charles Cresson Wood, Information Security Policies Made Easy Version 9, (Pentasafe, 2002).[77]

Peltier, Thomas, Information Security Policies and Procedures: A Practitioner's Reference, Second Edition (Auerbach Publications, 2004)

Peltier, Thomas, Policies and Procedures for Data Security: A Complete Manual for Computer Systems and Networks (CRC Press, 2017)

I've read others but will not list them here. Have a book to suggest? Let me know.

Other additional reading

More may be listed on my website.

---

[75] Please see the prior footnote about whether to consider purchasing these yourself.
[76] I am grateful to Professor Bel Raggad for his book and guidance.
[77] Note that the current version seems to be version 14, and does not seem to be a book for purchase anymore but a licensing agreement at $1,200 per year. It no longer seems to list Mr. Wood as the author, but indicates it remains based upon his work.

26

Policy checklist

Big picture

Policy and procedure documents should accomplish a few general tasks:

- Help the organization accomplish its mission
- Keep the organization in compliance with many legal requirements
- Protect the organization (especially when the topic is cybersecurity).

Your checklist

Here's a checklist, with major sections in bold.

1. **Gather initial information and summarize (before your first read-through)**
2. Full name of governance document, e.g.
   a. Information Security and/or Cybersecurity Policy
   b. Incident Response Plan
   c. Privacy Policy
   d. Information Security Standards
   e. Etc.
3. Filename of document
4. Approval date (or other relevant dates)
5. Summarize the primary purposes of document
6. Summarize the intended audiences (e.g. all employees, selected employees, customers/clients/consumers, regulators, insurance, etc.)
7. Summarize the length (e.g. pages, words) and level of detail. How long a read do you think it is? (average reading time is 200-250 words per minute)
8. Summarize information about current version, who manages it, who implements it, who approved it, etc.
9. Are there initial concerns expressed regarding the document? (e.g. from organization, regulator, etc.)

10. What laws and regulations apply to the organization relating to this document?
11. **First read-through and initial questions**
    Read through the policy one time, all the way through
12. Summarize your initial impression after reading it through once.
13. Summarize your initial questions after reading through it once.
14. Overall, is the document helpful, practical, clear, and current?
15. How long did it take you to read it?
16. Does it establish the internal rules we want the organization and employees to follow?
17. Is it helpful for the organization and employees?
18. Is it the right compromise between length and brevity, generality and specificity?
19. **Cross reference part 1**
20. Does it align with relevant external rules (laws/regulations)? Where appropriate, does it name them?
21. Does it align with helpful external guidance? Where appropriate, does it name them or point to additional resources?
22. Is it consistent with other internal documentation? Does it point to relevant internal resources?
23. Is there anything that conflicts with external rules, best practices, or other internal rules?
24. **Details and specifics**
25. Does the document name adequately describe the subject matter?
26. Does the document name properly describe the type of governance document this is? (e.g. policy, standard, procedure, plan). The substance should properly match the name. E.g. a policy should be more general, a procedure should be more detailed, etc.
27. Is length and level of detail appropriate for purpose and audience?
28. Is versioning information readily available, including revision and approval date?
29. Has it been reviewed or updated recently?
30. Is the review/update history apparent or otherwise available?
31. Does it indicate who is responsible for maintaining, implementing, and approving the document?
32. Does it establish or identify internal governance mechanisms?
33. Does it indicate the classification of the document? (e.g., confidential, internal use only, public)
34. Overall, is the document helpful, practical, clear, and current?
35. Is it readable and understandable for intended audiences?

36. Is it written clearly?
37. Is it practical?
38. Is it well-organized?
39. Is it modular?
40. Are important points stated clearly and properly emphasized?
41. Does the document establish rules for employees to follow, and that there could be discipline for failing to follow those rules?
42. **Input, advice, and stakeholders**
43. Did it need or obtain a legal review?
44. Did it need input and review from relevant stakeholders, employees, and departments?
45. Did it need and receive review and input from experts in the subject?
46. Did it need and receive review and input from relevant members of the intended audience, including those charged with implementing it?
47. Did it receive input and support from higher level management?
48. **Implementation**
49. Has it been read by appropriate members of the organization?
50. Do employees need training on the document?
51. Does the organization need to receive an acknowledgement from each employee that they read the document and will abide by it?
52. Is it followed by the organization and relevant members?
53. Is there any doubt within the organization or by employees as to whether the document is in effect and enforced? In other words, does anyone believe the document is just "on paper" or "for show" but not really in effect?
54. **Cross reference part 2 - Big picture of internal governance**
55. Is this document the right length and scope compared to other internal governance documents which may be related?
    a. Should documents be split or merged? For example, maintaining or navigating a single, large governance document can be burdensome, but so can maintaining or navigating dozens of separate, shorter governance documents.
    b. Grouping appropriate subjects together reduces the number of documents, assuming document length is manageable.
    c. Keeping policies general means less frequent revisions are needed, and reduces the burden on high-level management to review and approve.

    d. Keeping procedures specific ensures more frequent changes can be done and at a lower level of approval than a policy.
56. Is governance document review and update an integrated component of organization management, such that documents accurately reflect management directives?
57. Other matters?
58. Consider other details or general areas not listed above. No policy is perfect, and neither is any checklist (including this one).

References

- This book
- Policy checklist, https://johnbandler.com/policy-checklist/

27

Quick start guide

If your new TV has a quick start guide then this book can too.

I know some people want to read the CliffsNotes or TLDR[78] version so I created this guide.

If you want all the details, read the book all the way through.

Here are quick summaries of important points and where in the book to find more.

1. Good governance documents (policies, procedures, etc.) serve important purposes.

They

- Help the organization accomplish its mission
- Keep the organization in compliance with legal requirements
- Protect the organization.

They are never just for show. They have legal significance and should be referred to, followed, and updated when needed.

For more, see Chapter 8 on the ideal governance document and Part 1 on the Five Components for Policy Work.

2. Governance documents should be created and updated with a solid process.

This process can ensure quality documents are built and improve people and the organization along the way.

---

[78] CliffsNotes bills themselves as the "the original (and most widely imitated) study guide." https://cliffsnotes.com/discover-about

   TLDR stands for "too long; didn't read" and is sometimes used—in seeming contradiction—before a quick summary.

This process considers the Five Components of Policy Work, including:

- Mission (business goals)
- External rules (laws, regulations, etc.)
- Practice (action)
- Internal rules (policies, procedures, etc.)
- External guidance (best practices, etc.)

For more, there is a point on each below, also see Chapter 2 on the Five Components.

3. The process of building and updating governance documents should include some degree of planning and project management.

In other words, find the happy medium between doing zero planning and management, and adding excessive burdens to yourself and others.

When you have time to plan and learn about project management, read Chapter 9 on project management basics, and Chapter 11 on document project basics.

4. When you have "no time to plan", remember these golden rules:

- Consider your deadline and there is at least some time available to you for planning
- Triage your tasks and priorities accordingly
- Try to make a small improvement
- Do no harm. Remember the document you put in place will have legal significance and become the status quo.
- Plan now for next time. Take 30 seconds to put calendar items in place for the next cycle.

See the short Chapter 10 on Planning, shmanning (when there is no time to plan).

5. Mission. Every rule should exist to help serve the mission.

Ultimately, this can come down to ensuring the organization is healthy, compliant, and bringing in revenue.

Take a few minutes to ensure you can justify the policy on the mission and business needs arena and justify any tensions or balance between compliance and mission.

Mission comes first but you may already know your organization's mission so you can probably do this quickly.

For more, see Chapter 4 on Mission.

6. External rules must be considered ⚠

Every organization needs to comply with various legal requirements, and governance documents are an important part of that compliance. The motivation for policies often has a strong compliance focus.

Research and document what laws, regulations, contracts, and legal norms (including the law of negligence) apply to the policy project.

This is important, so give it sufficient priority.

For more on this, see Chapter 5 on external rules.

7. Practice and action need to be considered

Sometimes policy work is motivated by a need to improve employee practices that are deficient or non-compliant. Consider what these might be and how to correct them.

Policy work should also consider what practices are good and how to ensure they continue even when personnel change.

For more on this, see Chapter 6 on practice and action.

8. External guidance is important too

Consider what best practices there are in your industry, which you should follow, whether and how you should adjust or adapt them.

Consider guidance from government agencies regarding laws that apply to your organization.

Consider guidance on how to do governance document work (including this book).

For more on this, see Chapter 7 on external guidance.

9. Organize your documents and process

Take some time to organize your documents and processes to ensure that they move forward efficiently. This includes using good file naming techniques on the document, and include the version date within the filename. For example:

XYZ Cybersecurity Policy v6 2024-08-01 DRAFT.docx

Clearly denote a draft document is a "draft" both within the document and in the filename.

When you distribute a document, take a minute to include the document name and a clear summary. For example:

> *Here is the latest draft policy, attached with filename:*
> *XYZ Cybersecurity Policy v6 2024-08-01 DRAFT.docx*
>
> *This version includes [SUMMARIZE BRIEFLY]*

Use your word processor's features for tracking changes and comments.

More details in Chapter 16 on managing the documents.

10. Remember that governance documents are by people, for people and affect people.

So don't forget the human element.

Keep in mind that people have different backgrounds, understandings, motivations, may be invested in certain things or protecting their turf or trying to avoid taking on new tasks.

More on this in Chapter 12 on people.

11. Someone will approve that document, keep them in the loop

Try to keep the approver(s) in the loop throughout the process, and remember that they are either on the project team or are informed or consulted throughout the project.

Last minute disapproval or changes by the approver that are not properly discussed can negate prior careful project work.

More on this in Chapter 17.

12. When a document is approved it needs to be finalized, distributed, and notification or training needs to be done.

It is not "shelf-ware" but an important instrument of the organization to be referred to, followed, and updated as needed,

For more on the process after approval, see Chapter 18 on publication, training, implementation.

Then see Chapter 22 using, maintaining, and updating the policies.

13. Policies (like life) are about decision making.

Everyone makes decisions differently and prioritizes different things. Try to use facts, law, logic and common sense to make good policy decisions that are defensible and justifiable.

See Chapter 14 for more on risk and decision making.

14. There is no perfect way to write a governance document or conduct the document project.

Or even to manage an organization. Consider best practices and adapt them and find what works for you within your organization.

Some organizations and people have a deficiency of planning or formality and could benefit from greater focus on this.

Some may have an excess of formality and bureaucracy and could benefit from more spontaneity and flexibility.

Find what works for you and your organization.

15. Take some time to improve the organization, yourself, and the project team

Policies are both a process and a destination. The process matters.

Writing can be hard, law and legal requirements can be hard, people can be hard. Take some time to learn how to navigate all these areas better. Improve your knowledge, improve how you do things.

16. Rushing this document project?

Resolve to have more time to plan and conduct the project next time.

Next time, spend a little more time in the book, on planning, and on executing that document project.

John Bandler

28

My journey to write this book

- Few people read books on policies and procedures
- Fewer people write a book on policies and procedures
- Even fewer people want to read about *why* someone wrote such a book
  - That's why I stuck this in the back
- Here's how this book came to be

Rules and instructions are all around us, including from the people we work for, signs we see, and more. My journey to write this book started over thirty years ago, even if I didn't know it until recently.

Once upon a time I was in Army Reserve Officers' Training Corps (ROTC) and—as you can imagine—the Army has a lot of rules and instructions. Not all of them were written well or conveyed pleasantly but I appreciated their necessity (mostly) then and now.

Upon my start in the New York State Police I had six months of free room and board at the academy in Albany. There were many rules and orders which ranged from policies and procedures of the organization (a field manual, administrative manual, interim orders, memos, lectures, shouting, and more) plus the state's penal law, criminal procedure law, and vehicle and traffic law. The next eight years in the organization meant applying lots of laws and rules to investigate crime, incidents, and accidents.

Eventually I went to law school and learned a lot more about laws, rules, and processes.

I graduated from law school and became a prosecutor at the New York County (Manhattan) District Attorney's Office. I was lucky to be hired there, and by the legendary Robert Morgenthau no less. In my thirteen years there I saw that criminal prosecution is a process of applying many legal steps to investigate a crime, charge someone with a crime, and then resolve that litigation.

Then I entered private practice and I now work with organizations to improve and build their policies and procedures. Writing is important to convey the rules, comply with the law, and accomplish the mission. When I serve clients, I know the importance of what they put in writing.

I built an online course on cybersecurity policies and procedures and researched extensively for that. I read many other books on policies and procedures, many of which had helpful thoughts and informed my course and thought processes. But some were lacking, and in the back of my mind, I felt I could create a book on policies that could help every organization.

As I serve clients and teach students, my research continues, and I refine and build my resources.

This is my third book. The two before were a learning process, and I have written dozens of articles, hundreds if you count my website. I know the writing process can be difficult and I have learned a lot about it.

I have taught hundreds of students, and this means reviewing their written submissions–weekly assignments and then final papers. I know writing and law is a struggle for some and I try to encourage the effort so they will improve their writing and themselves.

I felt like all this experience and some of my thoughts can help you build better policies and procedures for your organization. And realize that both the process and product can improve the team and the organization. That you can improve yourself, your knowledge of law, and your ability to write and communicate. Maybe it will help you achieve personal success (however you define that term), rise in your organization, or lead your organization to greater achievement.

With my prior two books, I was lucky to have reputable and good publishers and editors, and as involved as I was much of the process was beyond my control. What if I could do it all myself and bring the book to publication quickly and then update it whenever I wanted?

Writing this book has been its own journey and I have learned more about all the things involved, and there have been many choices and much work on both substance, style, and process. I'm glad I took this trip and hope my efforts show.

29

List of diagrams

I created these diagrams, which are largely an evolution of diagrams I created for my website and that I use for teaching students and clients, and for my online courses. I hope they help convey the concepts.

- Five Components for Policy Work with external guidance highlighted, 49
- ENTER, five steps for governance documents, 66
- SOW: statement of work and scope of work, 71
- Good policies and a good policy process support the triad, 95
- Cybersecurity and privacy law (2), 163
- Bandler's Four Pillars of Cybersecurity, 180
- Internal rules platform cross section (unwritten and written rules) (reprise), 190

The diagrams were prepared using PowerPoint.

The cover was prepared using Publisher.

My wife provided valuable guidance on appearance and style on everything.

30

Index

H

Handbook, 10, 22, 64, 94, 115
Harm
  as part of risk management, 110-110, 113
  "do no harm", 24, 77, 81, 212
Homo Sapiens, *see* People
Hopeless pursuit, *see* Wild goose chase
Human resources, 6, 33, 40, 55, 64, 94
Humans, *see* People

I

Implementation (of new document), 153-157 (Chapter 18), 209, 214
Incorporation documents, 23, 115
Index, you found it!
Information assets, 33, 35-36, 162, 171, 180, 199
Information governance, 6, 36, 175-176, 199
Information security, 30, 40, 54, 89, 161-162, 199
  frameworks, 171-176 (Chapter 20)
  see also Cybersecurity
Insurance, 43, 110, 111, 165,
  cyberinsurance, 165
Internal rules, 9, 10, 12, 21-30 (Chapter 3), 144, 199 (and most of the book)
  analysis of, 115
  internal guidance compared, 59

J

Johnbandler.com, 199 (and where QR codes in the book will take you)
Judge made law, 42

L

Law, 9, 12, 13, 14, 24, 37-47 (Chapter 5), 95, 115-116, 199
  cybersecurity law, 161-169 (Chapter 19)
  see also External rules, Compliance
Lawsuit, 7, 33, 130, 189
Lawyer, 15, 19, 38-40, 44-45, 54, 59, 93, 117
  see also Attorney

M

Magnitude of harm, 110, 111
Management, 4, 6, 9, 23, 25, 33, 34, 199
  document management, 129-145 (Chapter 16)
  management tone, 63-64
  project management, 69-73 (Chapter 9)
  risk management, 109-112
  see also Governance
Manual, 13, 23
Mission, 3, 9, 15, 31-36 (Chapter 4), 95, 104, 114-115
  Fourth platform of Mission, 15-17
  mission vs. compliance, 17-18
Mistakes in the book, if you find one, it is an Easter Egg (but let me know).
Morgenthau, Robert, 217

N

Negligence, 36, 38, 42, 43, 46, 116, 163, 164
NIST Cybersecurity Framework (CSF), 60, 173, 174-176, 179
Noncompliant organization, 14, 15, 22

O

Operations, 69-70, 81, 182, 188, 200
Organization, 3, 200
  internal rules of, 9, 10, 12, 21-30
    (Chapter 3), 144, 199 (and most of
    the book)
  mission of, 3, 9, 15, 31-36 (Chapter
    4), 95, 104, 114-115
  noncompliant organization, 14, 15,
    22

P

Payment Card Industry Data Security
  Standard (PCI-DSS)
PCI DSS, 165, 172, 174
People, 66-67, 72, 85-95 (Chapter 12),
  200
Personnel department, *see* Human
  resources
Pillars, 200
  see Four Pillars of Cybersecurity
Planning, 102, 121
  backwards planning, 80, 197
  document project planning, 79-84
    (Chapter 11)
  when there is no time to plan, 75-77
    (Chapter 10)
Plans (document types), 22, 71, 101
Platform analogy, 22, 26, 190
Platform, *see* Three Platforms to
  Connect and Fourth Platform to
  Connect
Policies and Procedures, 1-220
Policy (policies), as a specific type of
  rule, 22, 26, 200
Policy checklist, 207-210 (Chapter
  26)
Portfolio, 70, 200
Practice (action), 9, 12, 49-52
  (Chapter 6), 116, 200
  see also External guidance (best
    practices)
Precedent, 42

Privacy, 6, 8, 34, 36, 45-47, 163-164,
  165, 166, 167-169, 200
Probability of harm, 110, 111
Procedure (as a specific type of rule),
  22, 26, 115, 201
Program, 69-70, 114, 201
  cybersecurity program, 164, 173
Project life cycle, 73
Project management, 69-73 (Chapter
  9), 201
  see also Document project
    management
Project manager 4, 72, 73, 133, 148,
  149
Project, 201 (defined)
  document project basics, *see* Part 2
Publication (of new policies), 153-157
  (Chapter 18)
Pyramid, 25-26, 201

Q

QR code, 8

R

Redline, 107, 148, 149
Regulation, 9, 10, 12, 13, 14, 24, 37-
  47 (Chapter 5), 95, 115-116
  cybersecurity law, 161-169 (Chapter
    19)
  see also Law and External rules
Risk management, 6, 109-112, 175,
  181, 201
Risk mitigation, 110
Risk transfer, 110
Risk, 95, 109-112, 143, 149, 175-176,
  201
  see also Risk management and
    Decision making
Rules platform, *see* Internal rules,
  External Rules, Platform
Rules pyramid, 25-26

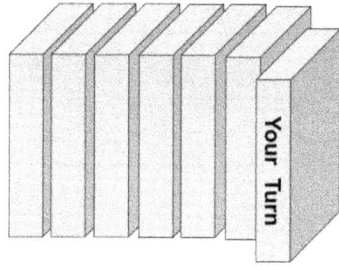

Part 7

Your turn

A few pages for your notes

When you run out of pages you can always buy another copy of the book! ☺

(Remember to check for an updated edition)

John Bandler

Policies and Procedures for Your Organization

_____

_____

_____

_____

_____

_____

_____

_____

_____

_____

_____

_____

_____

_____

_____

_____

_____

_____

_____

_____

_____

_____

www.ingramcontent.com/pod-product-compliance
Lightning Source LLC
Chambersburg PA
CBHW071726200326
41519CB00021BC/6589